THE WORLD'S GREATEST
GOLF COURSES

THE WORLD'S GREATEST
GOLF COURSES

A comprehensive guide to golf courses around the world

Geoffrey Giles

Bath · New York · Singapore · Hong Kong · Cologne · Delhi · Melbourne

First published by Parragon in 2009

Parragon
Queen Street House
4 Queen Street
Bath BA1 1HE, UK

Created and produced by JOLLANDS EDITIONS
Design JC LANAWAY
Course maps COMPARE INFOBASE LIMITED

ISBN 978-1-4075-7434-9

Printed in Malaysia

FRONT COVER *Turnberry Ailsa Course (Getty Images).*
BACK COVER *Golf ball on golf course, close-up, Saipan,
USA (Getty Images).*

PRACTICAL DETAILS

Most of the courses in this book welcome visiting golfers, the exceptions being some private clubs, mainly in the United States and Canada. The famous championship courses are inundated with requests to play so book well in advance. Club websites will usually include details of fees, availability, handicap restrictions, dress codes, and whether a letter of introduction is required, and many will have an online booking facility.

Distances in the book are given in yards, which are used in North America and – still, despite metrication – by the golfing community in Great Britain.

Scorecards give the hole lengths from the back or championship tees as they were at the time of writing. Note that, for championships, what might be a short par 5 for the members is sometimes re-designated as a long par 4 for competitors. Clubs frequently build new tees or simply remeasure their course, so these distances should only be used as a guideline.

Every effort has been made to check facts thoroughly, but errors may have crept in. The publisher would be grateful for corrections or information helpful for future editions.

▶▶▶ Contents

6 INTRODUCTION

 1 8–45
GREAT BRITAIN
& IRELAND

 2 46–61
NORTH
AMERICA

 3 62–65
CENTRAL &
SOUTH AMERICA

 4 66–77
CONTINENTAL
EUROPE

 5 78–83
MIDDLE EAST
& AFRICA

 6 84–95
ASIA &
AUSTRALASIA

96 INDEX
96 ACKNOWLEDGEMENTS

►►► Introduction

It was the great English-born American golf course designer Robert Trent Jones who wrote, 'The first golf course architect, of course, was the Lord, and he was the best there has ever been.' The early golfers of Scotland and the Netherlands played their golf on relatively undefined patches of ground wherever they happened to live. There was no such thing as a typical golf course. And while a few elements of a course have become standardized, there is still no standard golf course.

The Scots became the defining influence on golf when the Honourable Company of Edinburgh Golfers laid down the first set of rules in 1744. In 1754 twenty-two 'Noblemen and Gentlemen' gathered in St Andrews to form the Royal and Ancient Golf Club of St Andrews (R&A), and the newcomers gradually gained the ascendancy. Their rules dealt mainly with the situations that might occur during the course of a match – the rules of matchplay. You played against each other, not against the course. Medal play would have been unthinkable, because the number of holes per course varied until St Andrews, which had now reduced its course to one of 18 holes, standardized this number for a round of golf in 1858.

In the mid-19th century men began to 'design' golf courses. The great players of the day were called upon to lay out the 'links' of newly formed golf clubs. Those great players were all Scottish and they all played on the links courses of Scotland, on that strip of unfertile, sandy soil between the beach and the town or farmland. Inevitably they tried to recreate the features that gave their home courses distinction. They looked for green sites in hollows, which would be self-watering with dew, or on humps and hillocks, because they tested technique. Sand exposed by sheep sheltering from the wind or natural erosion had become a common feature of links, and these were replicated by early bunkers.

ABOVE Cape Kidnappers, New Zealand – an example of the work of American designer Tom Doak. Doak has an unerring talent for locating stunning green sites and keeping the golfer thinking until the very last putt has dropped.

Today's golf course designers are master craftsmen, and they are doing just what Allan Robertson, Tom Morris and Willie Park did a century and a half ago. They now have the benefit of computer-aided design, sophisticated earth-moving machines, real-estate lawyers, civil engineers and environmentalists. Given the restraints of what they may be allowed to do, ecologically, and the dire consequences of getting it the tiniest bit wrong, we should rejoice that the greatest players of our day are prepared to emulate Robertson, Morris and Park.

St Andrews

The Old Course, St Andrews, Fife, Scotland

St Andrews

There is no more famous golfing town than St Andrews. It is, after all, the Home of Golf, and the game has been played there since the 15th century. Overlooking the Old Course is the handsome clubhouse of the Royal and Ancient Golf Club (R&A), a comparative newcomer to St Andrews having been founded in 1754. Nowadays the R&A governs the game throughout the world, with the exception of North America, and every five years it brings its Open Championship (or British Open, as it is widely known through the golfing world) to the Old Course, producing winners of the calibre of Tiger Woods, Jack Nicklaus, Severiano Ballesteros and Nick Faldo in recent years and James Braid and Bob Jones in the distant past.

Jones was one of many golfers who found that it takes time to appreciate the many subtleties of the Old Course. It has humps and hollows here, there and everywhere; hundreds of bunkers, many in the unlikeliest of places, some such as Hell, Strath, Hill or Road terrifying even the world's greats; huge, rolling greens, all but four of them double greens shared by holes playing in opposite directions; and a wealth of history in every blade of grass – all the greats of golf have played here and the locals will recount tales fantastical of derring-do and catastrophe everywhere on the course. The first-time visitor would be well advised to employ the services of a good local caddie, not only to unravel the mysteries of playing the Old Course but also to share in some of those numerous St Andrews legends.

BOBBY JONES AND ST ANDREWS

Strange to relate, Bobby Jones hated the Old Course on his first visit, tearing up his card during the 1921 Open Championship, but he came to love it as he got to know it better, eventually saying, 'I could take out of my life everything except my experiences at St Andrews and I'd still have a rich, full life.' It was on the Old Course in 1930 that Jones won the Amateur Championship, defeating Roger Wethered 7 and 6. In this remarkable year Jones also won the US Amateur at Merion, the US Open at Interlachen and the Open Championship at Royal Liverpool, a feat unlikely to be repeated, now referred to as the Impregnable Quadrilateral. At the end of that season Jones, at the age of 28, retired from competitive golf, concentrating on his career as a lawyer.

CARD OF THE COURSE

Hole	Distance (yards)	Par
1	376	4
2	453	4
3	397	4
4	480	4
5	568	5
6	412	4
7	390	4
8	175	3
9	352	4
Out	3,603	36
10	380	4
11	174	3
12	348	4
13	465	4
14	618	5
15	456	4
16	423	4
17	455	4
18	357	4
In	3,676	36
Total	7,279	72

LEFT *One of the most famous views in golf, looking over the Swilcan Bridge towards the clubhouse of the R&A.*

BELOW RIGHT *The Road bunker is one of the most feared on the Old Course. Many great players settle for a bogey five rather than risk failing to escape its clutches.*

In the footsteps of the great

There is no simpler drive in golf than that on the 1st hole of the Old Course, or that would be the case if the tee were anywhere else than right in front of the R&A clubhouse. It is a hugely broad fairway shared with the 18th, and there are no bunkers. However, there is the sinuous Swilcan Burn to be cleared to reach the green. Thereafter the course makes its way out in the shape of a shepherd's crook to the Eden Estuary, turning in a loop before retracing its steps alongside the outward holes on wide shared fairways and greens. The space, which appears to invite uninhibited driving and cavalier approach play, is deceptive. Such are the ingenuities of the course's defences that how the hole is played from tee to green depends on exactly where the pin is located.

However much you may be enjoying your round you cannot relax until you have passed the 17th, the Road Hole, dominated by the treacherous Road bunker. Get in there and there may be no escape! But all is surely alleviated by the walk up the 18th, the most famous walk in golf.

'Without a doubt, I like it best of all the Open venues. It is my favourite course in the world.'

TIGER WOODS, OPEN CHAMPION AT
ST ANDREWS IN 2000 AND 2005

BUNKERS – THE STORIES BEHIND THE NAMES

It is said that there are 112 bunkers on the Old Course, which seems a conservative estimate to anyone who has played there. Some of them are in such obscure places that you could never imagine golfers getting into them – but they have! Most also have names. These are some of the more colourful:

CHEAPE'S (2ND HOLE) Named after the Cheape family that owns the nearby Strathtyrum estate. Sir James Cheape bought the Old Course in 1821 to save it from rabbit farmers. His son later sold it to the R&A which, in turn, sold it to the town. Golfers owe Sir James an enormous debt of gratitude.

CARTGATE (3RD HOLE) Shares its name with the hole itself, so called because of the former cart track that crossed the hole towards the beach.

GINGER BEER (4TH HOLE) Again, a name shared with the hole, referring back to the mid-19th century when 'Old Daw' Anderson set up a ginger beer stall there.

SUTHERLAND (4TH/15TH HOLE) Sutherland should not be a factor on the 4th were it not for the difficulties of the right-hand side of the fairway often forcing golfers too far to the left. It was named after one A. G. Sutherland who is reputed to have had the bunker re-excavated when it was filled in in the 1860s.

COTTAGE (4TH/15TH HOLE) For the same reasons as Sutherland, Cottage should not be a factor on the 4th, but it is. It refers to Pilmour Cottage, which once stood nearby and is now the clubhouse of the Eden Course.

STUDENTS (4TH HOLE) There are two theories behind the naming of these bunkers. It has been said that they refer to the practice of busy students, not having the time for a full round, playing out this far and then turning for home. An alternative suggestion is that these were cosy (and out-of-sight) places for male students to take their lady friends.

SPECTACLES (4TH HOLE) This is exactly what they look like, set at the foot of the ridge crossing this fairway.

COFFINS (6TH/13TH HOLES) You are playing a little extravagantly if you get in these on the 6th hole. They are a threat to all, however, on the 13th. They are so coffin-like that you feel you may be in them forever.

SHELL (7TH HOLE) Apart from the fact that it looks rather like a mussel shell from above, the name refers back to the days when the base of the bunker used to be cockle shells. (If you are wildly off course on the 7th, you might find yourself in Hill or Strath bunkers – leave these for the 11th!)

SHORT HOLE BUNKER (8TH HOLE) Some of the bunker names are rather more prosaic!

KRUGER (9TH HOLE) This is actually two bunkers, built during the Boer War and named after the former president of the Transvaal.

A third bunker, further on, is named Mrs Kruger. Rumour has it that there is also one named Kruger's Mistress!

STRATH (11TH HOLE) This commemorates the Strath brothers. Andrew won the 1865 Open Championship. His brother David tied for first place in 1876 but he refused to take part in the play-off, leaving Bob Martin as the champion.

HILL (11TH HOLE) Hill is not far behind Strath in venom. It is cut into the face of the hill on which the 11th green sits.

ADMIRAL'S (12TH HOLE) Sited close to the tee, the bunker is said to have been named after an admiral who, in his 80s, failed to see the sizeable bunker as he walked forward from the tee, distracted as he was by a beautiful young lady walking past, wearing, it is said, pillar-box red.

BELOW *Hell Bunker dominates strategy on the 14th hole for handicap golfers. Will the second shot clear it or do you go round the side of it?*

STROKE (12TH HOLE) Get in here and you almost certainly will drop a stroke.

NICK'S (13TH HOLE) The first of several bunkers threatening a pulled drive, presumably named after the devil who put it there.

CAT'S TRAP (13TH HOLE) Invisible from the fairway, the bunker catches your ball as a cat traps a mouse.

WALKINSHAW (13TH HOLE) Named after a local golfer who made a habit of visiting this pot bunker.

LION'S MOUTH (13TH HOLE) Lion's Mouth is another vicious bunker lying in wait beyond Cat's Trap. Perversely, Lion's Mouth is smaller than Cat's Trap.

THE BEARDIES (14TH HOLE) A quartet of bunkers with whiskery grass adorning their lips.

BENTY (14TH HOLE) Benty refers to one of the traditional seaside grasses: Bent.

KITCHEN (14TH HOLE) Kitchen was once known as the Devil's Kitchen because it was a small but deep pot bunker. It has since been enlarged.

HELL (14TH HOLE) One of the best-known bunkers in golf with a vast acreage and a seriously steep face from which escape forward is by no means guaranteed.

GRAVE (14TH HOLE) A small bunker in front of the green, which was formerly coffin-shaped.

PRINCIPAL'S NOSE (16TH HOLE) A set of three bunkers said to represent the prominent nose of the principal of St Mary's College in the mid-19th century. It is also said to be named after the ugly protuberance from the porch above the doorway of a principal's lodgings in the town.

DEACON SIME (16TH HOLE) Deacon Sime refers to a St Andrews clergyman who asked for his ashes to be scattered in the bunker, on the premise that he had spent so much of his earthly life in that particular bunker that he might as well spend eternity there as well.

GRANT'S (16TH HOLE) Commemorates a 19th-century captain of the R&A who made a habit of getting into this bunker.

WIG (16TH HOLE) Formerly called Jackson's Wig, recalling the formal dress of golfers in days past. Jackson was a captain of the R&A.

SCHOLAR'S (17TH HOLE) Scholar's is a reminder that the course used to be played in the opposite direction. You were a promising young scholar if you could clear this bunker with your drive.

PROGRESSING (17TH HOLE) You were doing well, but had not yet attained the proficiency of a scholar, if you could clear this bunker.

ROAD (17TH HOLE) The fearsome bunker that eats into the green of the Road Hole, both named after the tarmac road running tight along the right side of the green.

Carnoustie

Championship Course, Carnoustie Golf Links, Angus, Scotland

Is Carnoustie the toughest course on the Open Championship roster? The way it was prepared for the 1999 Open in the wind and rain it certainly was, Paul Lawrie's winning score being six over par. It was more sympathetically prepared for the 2007 Open, when Padraig Harrington and Sergio Garcia tied on 277, seven under par, Harrington winning in a four-hole play-off. What most observers were agreed on was that this set-up displayed all the greatness of this historic links, and in particular that there were often two or three different strategies for playing a particular hole, depending on a golfer's strengths and weaknesses, the wind and the weather.

It is not certain when golf began in Carnoustie (probably over 500 years ago) but it was some time around 1842 that Allan Robertson – the pre-eminent golfer at that time – was brought from St Andrews to lay out a ten-hole course on the Barry Links. Another St Andrews stalwart, Old Tom Morris, made considerable alterations in 1867, expanding the course to 18 holes, and James Braid made the final significant changes in 1926.

The longest Open Championship course

Carnoustie hosted its first Open Championship in 1931, with Scottish-born American Tommy Armour coming from five behind to win – subsequent champions have included Henry Cotton (1937), Ben Hogan (1953), Gary Player (1963) and Tom Watson (1975). As a championship course Carnoustie has always been among the longest. For the 2007 Open it measured a daunting 7,412 yards/6,778 m, the longest ever, with two par 4s reaching almost 500 yards/457 m in length, yet such is the prowess of contemporary professionals with modern equipment that many forsook their drivers, taking long irons from the tee. They did it for the simple reason that you cannot blast your way round this course. You have to plot your way around it. The bunkers are deep, gathering and perfectly positioned; the rough can be savage; out-of-bounds threatens on several holes; and the Jockie's and Barry burns were brilliantly incorporated into the design, especially on the last two holes.

Jockie's Burn, for instance, limits the length of the tee shot on the challenging 5th, putting pressure on the approach to a multi-level, snaking green, cunningly bunkered and over 50 yards/46 m deep. Out-of-bounds waits to wreck scores on the long 6th, causing many an errant tee shot to be pushed into the deep rough on the other side.

Of all the hazards it is the Barry Burn that is most feared, very largely because it comes into play viciously on the last two holes, hard on the heels of the 16th, a seriously long par 3 on which only the straightest of tee shots can pierce the bunkered mounds guarding the front of the green. Birdies here are rare, dropped shots frequent. The 17th then strikes out over the burn, which meanders hugely, creating almost an island fairway, with length restricted where the burn crosses the fairway.

Still to come is the scariest drive of them all, back over the Barry Burn to another narrow fairway, once again bounded by the burn. Even after a successful drive, there remains the long second to the green, which lies perilously close to the out-of-bounds fence and is, naturally, only just beyond yet another meander of the dreaded burn. What a tough hole!

LEFT *Barry Burn, snaking across the 17th and 18th. Jean van de Velde's skirmishes with it cost him a seven in the 1999 Open Championship, when a six would have won it.*

CARD OF THE COURSE

Hole	Distance (yards)	Par
1	406	4
2	463	4
3	358	4
4	412	4
5	415	4
6	578	5
7	410	4
8	183	3
9	478	4
Out	3,703	36
10	466	4
11	383	4
12	499	4
13	176	3
14	514	5
15	472	4
16	248	3
17	461	4
18	499	4
In	3,718	35
Total	7,421	71

▶ Almost 300 young men from Carnoustie and the surrounding area have emigrated to the United States to work as golf professionals. One of the best known was Stewart Maiden, Bobby Jones's teacher at the East Lake Club, Atlanta.

▶ The Smith brothers from Carnoustie had an enviable professional record. Alex was twice US Open champion, Willie once, and Macdonald came second to Bobby Jones in both the British Open and the US Open in 1930.

▶ Ben Hogan, one of golf's all-time greats, entered only one British Open, in 1953 at Carnoustie. He won the championship by four strokes. It was part of a remarkable run of victories that included the US Masters and the US Open.

'I love playing over here because it allows you to be creative.'

TIGER WOODS

Gleneagles

Gleneagles

King's Course, Gleneagles Hotel, Auchterarder, Perthshire, Scotland

When the 2014 Ryder Cup is played in Scotland it will be at Gleneagles. Jack Nicklaus's PGA Centenary Course has the honour of hosting it, having proved its fitness by hosting the annual Johnnie Walker Championship on the European Tour. The enormous hotel, built in the style of a French château and the venue for the 2005 G8 Summit, will then be exactly 90 years old.

ABOVE *The 7th on the King's Course is a tough dogleg on which the further you aim left to shorten the dogleg the longer you have to drive to clear a ridge.*

Older still are James Braid's two wonderful courses, opened before the hotel, in 1919. The King's and Queen's courses were a vital part of the strategy to attract royalty, nobility and the merely wealthy to the hotel, the pride and joy of the Caledonian Railway, which was described both as a 'Palace in the Glens' and as the 'Riviera in the Highlands'. Clearly the railway company's ambitions were well founded, for the hotel remains one of the world's great hotels to this day, and Braid's golf courses are as revered as ever.

Both the King's and the Queen's are serious contenders for the coveted title of the finest inland course in Scotland. Neither course is long enough seriously to challenge today's top players – hence the need for the construction of the PGA Centenary Course – but those who value charm, variety, subtlety and ingenuity in a golf course in ravishing surroundings can still derive great satisfaction from a round on either, preferably both. And, of course, they are maintained in impeccable condition.

CARD OF THE COURSE

Hole	Distance (yards)	Par
1	362	4
2	436	4
3	374	4
4	466	4
5	178	3
6	480	5
7	444	4
8	178	3
9	409	4
Out	3,327	35
10	499	5
11	230	3
12	442	4
13	464	4
14	309	4
15	459	4
16	158	3
17	377	4
18	525	5
In	3,463	36
Total	6,790	71

▶ The principal reason for the wonderful condition of the courses at Gleneagles is that they were built on the sand and gravel left behind when the ice from the Ice Age melted.

▶ 'The finest parcel of land in the world I have ever been given to work with,' is how Jack Nicklaus described the building of the PGA Centenary Course, venue for the 2014 Ryder Cup.

Challenging golf and uplifting scenery

On both courses each hole is named, in keeping with an old Scottish tradition, and at Gleneagles the holes were named from the outset, not carrying forward some ancient traditional name (for the holes were new) but quite simply to amuse visitors. Thus 'Drum Sichty' is no more than a view of the hills while 'Kittle Kink' is a tricky bend. But the names are good ice-breakers between player and caddie, and a good caddie is useful not only in guiding the player through the many problems posed by hilly courses, but also in sharing the finer points of Braid's clever designs with the appreciative golfer.

One of the great delights of the courses is the way the holes follow each other to create an integrated whole, with refreshing changes of pace, a good balance of challenges and a constant sense of development. At a little under 6,000 yards/5,486 m the Queen's Course may seem too short for the accomplished player, but do not be fooled! Seven of the par 4s exceed 400 yards/366 m in length and there are two substantial par 3s, the 14th and 17th. It was a favourite course of Lee Trevino.

In comparison with the Queen's, the King's is said to be more masculine. Sandy Lyle has particular respect for the tough, uphill 4th: in Lyle's opinion, 'a first-class hole by any standard'. Braid himself considered his favourite hole on the course to be the 13th, another long two-shot hole, appropriately named Braid's Brawest ('Braid's Best'). Everywhere there is a sense of space, the twists and turns of each course giving ever-changing views of the uplifting mountain scenery. These are not so much golf courses as experiences!

'If heaven is as good as this, I sure hope they have some tee times left.'

LEE TREVINO, REMARKING ON THE QUEEN'S COURSE

Muirfield

Muirfield

The Honourable Company of Edinburgh Golfers, Muirfield, Gullane, East Lothian, Scotland

Muirfield is the third home of the Honourable Company of Edinburgh Golfers, who from 1874 began to host the Open Championship in rotation with Prestwick and St Andrews. In 1891 they moved from Musselburgh to Muirfield, nearly 20 miles/32 km to the east of Edinburgh, calling on Old Tom Morris to lay out their new course.

Only a year after it opened Muirfield hosted its first (and the club's seventh) Open Championship. Fourteen further Opens have followed, as well as the Amateur Championship, Senior Open, Ryder Cup, Walker Cup and Curtis Cup. Some of the greatest names in golf have triumphed at Muirfield, including Vardon, Braid, Hagen, Cotton, Player, Nicklaus, Trevino, Watson, Faldo and Els – an impressive list.

Tom Morris's layout was unusual for its day in consisting of two contra-rotating loops of nine holes, one inside the other. This meant that the wind would blow from a different direction on almost every hole. The routing remains but little else of Morris's course survives, today's being mostly the work of Harry Colt and Tom Simpson in the 1920s.

BELOW Muirfield's 12th green is slightly raised, with downslopes and bunkers all around, and, as so often on this course, everything is visible as you play your shot.

THE OLDEST GOLF CLUB

Which is the oldest golf club in the world? Royal Blackheath in southeast London is known to have existed in 1608. Golf was certainly played in Scotland in 1457 because King James II of Scotland issued a decree prohibiting it. It was in the Edinburgh suburb of Leith that the Honourable Company first held a competition over its five-hole course in 1744. As the club's records are complete thereafter, the Honourable Company, which gave the game its first set of rules, becomes the oldest club with a complete, continuous history.

The fairest of tests

The course is well respected by the top players, particularly for its fairness – there is very little blindness and there are few capricious bounces. It is a notably good test of driving, the rough being particularly grasping, and some of its bunkering can only be described as ferocious! Perhaps of all the Open courses Muirfield has no 'stand-out' hole, for it is a very evenly distributed examination of the game, but most players would agree that the 6th, 8th and 18th are among the best long, two-shot holes in links golf. The 13th, too, is a white-knuckle short hole with a long, narrow green perched above five terrifying bunkers. A brilliant escape from one of these set up Ernie Els's Open win in 2002.

From the visitor's point of view, it is worth noting that the club does not introduce temporary tees or winter greens in the off season. You get to play the real course, and for a reduced green fee, to boot.

▶ Jack Nicklaus, after winning the 1966 Open, said, 'It is essentially a fair course. It has more definition than any links that the Open is played on.' He went on to name the first course he created – in Dublin, Ohio, USA – Muirfield Village.

▶ It was at Muirfield, in 1892, that the Open Championship was first played over 72 holes. Previously it had been over 36 holes. It was also at Muirfield in 1892 that an entrance fee to play in the Open Championship was first imposed.

▶ Ben Crenshaw (former US Masters champion and a distinguished golf course architect) praised Muirfield for 'its beautiful honesty as a test of golf'.

CARD OF THE COURSE

Hole	Distance (yards)	Par
1	448	4
2	351	4
3	378	4
4	213	3
5	560	5
6	468	4
7	185	3
8	443	4
9	508	5
Out	3,554	36
10	475	4
11	389	4
12	381	4
13	191	3
14	448	4
15	415	4
16	186	3
17	546	5
18	449	4
In	3,480	35
Total	7,034	71

'I liked it from the first day I played it.'

JACK NICKLAUS, ON WINNING THE 1966 OPEN CHAMPIONSHIP

Royal Dornoch

Royal Dornoch Golf Club, Dornoch, Sutherland, Scotland

'The most fun I ever had playing golf,' was Tom Watson's opinion of Royal Dornoch, an opinion shared by many of the famous golfers who have made the pilgrimage north to Dornoch. They have visited in large numbers because Dornoch is high on the must-play list of all who have an interest in golf course design.

Golf has been played at Dornoch for some 500 years. The present club, with a modest nine-hole course, was founded in 1877 but a more significant date in Dornoch's development was 1883, when John Sutherland was appointed secretary. He it was who brought in Old Tom Morris to extend the course to 18 holes in 1886; who subsequently refined and improved the design; who had the course brought into exemplary condition; who worked to have Dornoch created a Royal club; and who promoted Dornoch in his writings for London periodicals. Sutherland involved his professionals and greenkeepers in the development of the course and one of those was Donald Ross who subsequently emigrated to the United States where he introduced the concept of Dornoch-style raised greens to American golf design.

Remoteness is a blessing for Dornoch

Because Dornoch is so far from large centres of population it has never hosted important professional tournaments or the Open Championship. For that reason the course has been spared the incessant lengthening and alterations that are deemed necessary to keep modern professionals in check. Its holes remain as they were intended to be played twenty, thirty or even fifty years ago and the visitor today is still required to utilize a whole variety of types of pitch shot to gain access to these brilliantly sited greens. But it is not only on the approach shot that intelligent play is demanded, for the fairways use the natural slopes, humps and hollows cleverly, calling for precise and thoughtful driving. The wind, too, must be taken into account.

RIGHT *The delightful 10th hole at Dornoch, a gentle enough par 3 if you find the green from the tee, but the very devil if you miss.*

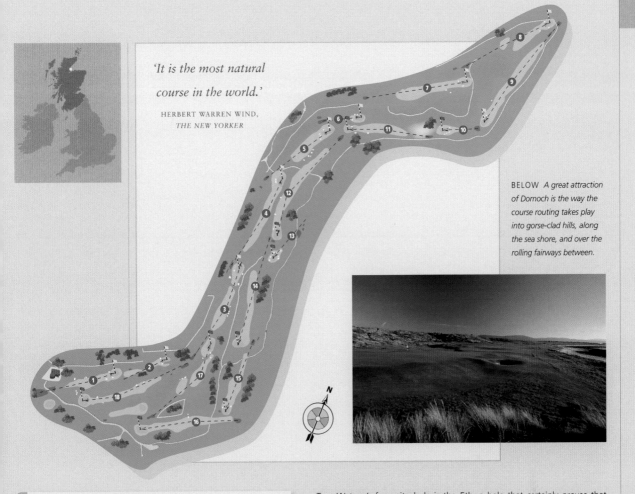

'It is the most natural

course in the world.'

HERBERT WARREN WIND,
THE NEW YORKER

BELOW *A great attraction
of Dornoch is the way the
course routing takes play
into gorse-clad hills, along
the sea shore, and over the
rolling fairways between.*

CARD OF THE COURSE

Hole	Distance (yards)	Par	Hole	Distance (yards)	Par
1	331	4	10	177	3
2	184	3	11	450	4
3	414	4	12	507	5
4	427	4	13	180	3
5	354	4	14	445	4
6	163	3	15	358	4
7	463	4	16	402	4
8	437	4	17	405	4
9	529	5	18	456	4
Out	3,302	35	In	3,380	35
			Total	6,682	70

Tom Watson's favourite hole is the 5th, a hole that certainly proves that excessive length is not essential for greatness. The view from the elevated tee is encouraging, the wide fairway some way below awaiting the drive. Yet the green is very long and angled significantly from left to right. The ideal drive, then, is down the left, but this is the side where trouble lurks in the form of a hill covered in gorse, threatening a lost ball. On the right the fairway slopes, guiding the ball inexorably towards a run of bunkers. Even if these are avoided the approach shot must be played across the axis of the narrow, kidney-shaped putting surface and there are further bunkers awaiting if that shot is overcooked.

Another of Dornoch's great holes is the bunkerless 14th – Foxy. Everything is governed by a series of dunes, which eat into the fairway from the right, obscuring the green from anywhere other than the extreme left of the fairway. The green is tucked round to the right behind the last of the dunes, broad but shallow, and raised sufficiently to make an approach shot from any length difficult to execute. The 17th, too, is a fine hole, sweeping downhill from the tee, then sharply up to a marvellously located green.

THE LURE OF DORNOCH

John Sutherland, the club's first secretary, was a considerable publicist for Dornoch, writing about it in the *London Daily News* and *Golf Illustrated*. But, unlike many of the great Scottish links that were located near railway lines, Dornoch had no railway until 1902. When the line opened, Sutherland lost no time in alerting golfers to take the overnight sleeper from London, to play the course the following morning. Among those who visited during these years were the Great Triumvirate, James Braid, Harry Vardon and J. H. Taylor. Taylor was so thrilled by the course that he arranged to take a fortnight's holiday in Dornoch every year while he was at the peak of his career, so perfect was the course for honing his game. Another visitor, much later, was Ben Crenshaw, who came to Dornoch as part of his preparations for the 1980 Open Championship, held that year at Muirfield. Asked, when he returned to Muirfield, what he thought of Dornoch he replied, 'Let me put it this way, I nearly did not come back.'

RIGHT *The 2nd at Dornoch looks benign enough from here, but get in the front right bunker and you may well have to escape sideways or backwards.*

Iain Lowe Photography

Royal Troon

Royal Troon

Royal Troon Golf Club, Troon, Ayrshire, Scotland

Troon was already an important sea port on the Firth of Clyde when a railway line was opened from Glasgow in 1840. Soon its beaches and clean air attracted Glaswegians to holiday there and the wealthy to build big houses. The next railway station south of Troon was Prestwick, the birthplace of championship golf, and in 1878 it was decided that Troon should have its own golf course.

Land was leased from the Duke of Portland and a five-hole course was created in the area where the present 1st, 2nd, 17th and 18th holes are. That course was extended piecemeal and by 1888 there were 18 holes, stretching to 5,600 yards/ 5,121 m, following much the same route as today's course. Further amendments took place through the years and by 1923 Troon was ready to host its first Open Championship.

Arnold Palmer was at the peak of his career when he won the Open Championship at Troon in 1962, yet even with his extraordinary powers of recovery he realized that he should 'not get locked into a life and death struggle with the course'. The first-time visitor, looking down the opening fairway from the tee, could be forgiven for querying that comment, for everything looks so straightforward and benign. And so it is, for a while.

Increasingly menacing

'As much by skill as by strength' is the club's motto, and the first three holes amble gently alongside the beach, each under 400 yards/366 m in length. Two birdieable par 5s are separated by a charming par 3 on top of the dunes, and everything seems pretty simple so far. The most inviting drive of the round follows at the 7th, but already the mind is sharpening for the mischief of the 8th, the notorious Postage

---

SOCIAL STATUS

At the end of the 1923 Open Championship the champion, Arthur Havers, and runner-up, Walter Hagen, were invited into the clubhouse for the presentation. Hagen refused to go as none of the professional golfers had been admitted to the clubhouse during the tournament. He went instead to the pub where a large number of the spectators joined him.

CARD OF THE COURSE

Hole	Distance (yards)	Par
1	361	4
2	391	4
3	379	4
4	558	5
5	210	3
6	599	5
7	403	4
8	123	3
9	423	4
Out	3,447	36
10	438	4
11	488	4
12	431	4
13	470	4
14	178	3
15	481	4
16	542	5
17	222	3
18	453	4
In	3,703	35
Total	7,150	71

▶ At the age of 71 Gene Sarazen played in the 1973 Open Championship at Troon and holed his tee shot on the Postage Stamp for an ace in the first round. In the second round he found a bunker off the tee, but holed his recovery shot.

LEFT *The Postage Stamp was originally played blind to a green on the far side of the dune. The new hole, built in 1909–10, was opened by Harry Vardon, James Braid, J. H. Taylor and Alex Herd.*

Stamp. It is the shortest hole in Open Championship golf, but you are either on the minuscule putting surface in one stroke, expecting a birdie, or else, if you missed the green, on a rough-clad hillock, in one of five deep greenside bunkers, or far below the green in a grassy hollow. Escape from any of these is no certainty, as the German player, Hermann Tissies, found to his cost in the 1950 Open. He finished up with a 15!

It is on the back nine, almost invariably played into the wind, that Troon bares its teeth, starting with an intimidating blind and angled drive to the elusive 10th fairway. The subsequent approach to a pinnacle green is difficult to judge. As for the 11th, it was described by Arnold Palmer as, 'The most dangerous hole I have ever seen.' The young Jack Nicklaus ran up a 10 on this hole in his first Troon Open, and during the 1997 Open the hole played to an average of 4.65 shots, easily the hardest on the course. Gorse and the hole's proximity to the railway line are the principal card wreckers.

The corrugated fairways of the 13th and 15th can be difficult to find and hold, the 17th is particularly tough in any sort of wind, and the 18th green is not one to overshoot, with the indignity of out-of-bounds immediately beyond the putting surface.

'The most dangerous hole
I have ever seen.'

ARNOLD PALMER,
DESCRIBING THE 11TH HOLE

Turnberry

Ailsa Course, Westin Turnberry Hotel, Turnberry, Ayrshire, Scotland

Turnberry's Ailsa Course enjoys the most spectacular setting of the half-dozen courses on the Open Championship roster. Often compared to California's Pebble Beach, it made its Open debut in 1977 and immediately produced a classic. Yet twice in its history this most majestic of courses was on the brink of extinction.

The railways played an important part in the spread of golf throughout Britain (America, too, for that matter). They were also responsible for the establishment of some of the country's finest hotels, not least Gleneagles, Cruden Bay and Turnberry. It was in the early 1900s that the Glasgow and South Western Railway negotiated a lease with the Marquis of Ailsa to enable them to construct a hotel at Turnberry. Already in existence on site was the Marquis's private 13-hole course, and a further 13 holes were added so that by 1906

Turnberry could, with justification, call itself a golf resort. It was good enough to host the British Ladies' Championship of 1912, and a promising future seemed certain.

Unfortunately progress was halted by World War I, when the course became an airfield. After that war restoration was undertaken and the thread of development resumed. Worse destruction came in 1939 in the form of a major air base, a vital part of the defence of transatlantic shipping lanes. Surely that was the end for Turnberry.

NAMING OF HOLES

In common with many Scottish courses, Turnberry's holes are named as well as numbered. The 2nd, for instance, is Mak Siccar ('make sure'), the 3rd Blaw Wearie ('out of breath'), 6th Tappie Tourie ('hit to the top'), 10th Dinna Fouter ('don't mess about'), 13th Tickly Tap ('a tricky little hit'), 15th Ca Canny ('take care'), 17th Lang Whang ('good whack').

LEFT *The short 11th, with the lighthouse and Ailsa Craig – the very essence of golf at Turnberry, a scene far removed from the runways of a wartime aerodrome.*

▶ In the final round of the 1979 European Open, played at Turnberry, Sandy Lyle birdied six of the first seven holes to establish an eight-shot lead, going on to win the tournament comfortably. The one hole he failed to birdie was the comparatively simple 2nd.

A remarkable resurrection

It was not the end, however, in the mind of Turnberry's manager, Frank Hole. Despite huge obstacles he managed to garner sufficient compensation from public funds after World War II and enough support from the newly formed British Railways, the hotel's owners, to turn three concrete runways and all their attendant paraphernalia into a fine golf course worthy of the investment. What Scottish designer Philip Mackenzie Ross produced was one of the most visually attractive courses in Britain.

Turnberry then worked its way up the tournament ladder and in 1977 it got its just reward – its first Open. It turned out to be one of the greatest Opens of all, the famous 'duel in the sun', with Tom Watson and Jack Nicklaus going head-to-head to produce some of the most spectacular golf ever seen, Watson just managing to hold out the battling Nicklaus in a thrilling contest.

It could be argued that the first three holes of the Ailsa Course sail under the radar a little, because the player is already anticipating the stretch of shoreline holes from the 4th to the 11th, unparalleled on Open Championship courses and worthy of comparison with those famed seaside holes at Pebble Beach. The seascapes are stunning, especially at sunset, but the golf requires full concentration, with a number of holes threaded down valleys between the dunes, others (such as the short 4th and 6th holes) fully exposed to the wind on top of the dunes. Arguably, the curving 8th is the best of these demanding par 4s, but the visitor cannot wait to be photographed on the peninsular 9th tee, the drive being made over enough of the ocean towards a distant clifftop fairway to cause trepidation in many an otherwise proficient player.

Perhaps the austerities of postwar Britain suggested to Ross a minimalist approach to bunkering, but this aspect was tightened in preparation for the 2009 Open, Turnberry's fourth. The second course, renamed Kintyre, has also been almost wholly remodelled by Donald Steel.

CARD OF THE COURSE

Hole	Distance (yards)	Par
1	350	4
2	430	4
3	462	4
4	165	3
5	442	4
6	231	3
7	529	5
8	431	4
9	454	4
Out	3,494	35
10	452	4
11	174	3
12	446	4
13	412	4
14	449	4
15	209	3
16	409	4
17	497	5
18	434	4
In	3,482	35
Total	6,976	70

The Belfry

Brabazon Course, The Belfry, Warwickshire, England

The Brabazon boasts a unique record – it is the only course on either side of the Atlantic to have hosted four Ryder Cups, with the Europeans winning in 1985 and 2002, the Americans winning in 1993, and the 1989 match halved. It has, then, been a happy hunting ground for the Europeans.

Driving past the courses (there are three) today, all you can see is a fairly unpromising, flat site with lines of parallel trees indicating where fairways might be located. Had you driven past before the courses were built you would not even have seen the trees, for these were potato fields on cold Midlands clay. The property had none of the qualities you would normally look for in assessing its suitability for golf, and golf of the highest class at that.

The job of creating a silk purse out of a sow's ear fell to Peter Alliss and Dave Thomas, and Thomas has returned over the years to make changes and tweaks to allow the course to keep pace with the prodigious advances in performance of golfers, golf clubs and golf balls, particularly over the past twenty years. Alliss and Thomas created a

workmanlike course of good length and plenty of challenge on a remarkably modest acreage.

For most of us the strategy of the Brabazon is about avoiding coming to grief in the many streams and lakes that enter into play on almost every hole. There is some prolific bunkering, too, not least on the short 7th, which, from the tee, suggests something out of Pine Valley. Card-wrecking holes come as early as the 3rd, a reachable par 5 (particularly from the everyday tees) with a corner of a lake to be carried on the way to the green, and we might even fall into the pond on the short 12th simply because it is there. But the holes that expose us all (amateur hacker and world star alike) are the 10th and 18th.

Two world-class holes

The 10th is a very short par 4, which actually gets better the shorter it is played. For the Ryder Cup it is reduced from its full 311 yards/284 m to around 270 yards/247 m. The reason is simple: to tempt the contestants to go for the green from the tee. You could get there with two 9-irons. But what would you not give for a putt for an eagle two? Get it wrong, of course, and you are fishing your ball out of the water or you have bounced off the branches of the green-side trees into perdition.

Perhaps the best is kept for last. This is one of the scariest drives in golf, those needing to attack the hole having to clear as much of the lake on the left as they dare. If that is successful, the second shot is played uphill over a further stretch of lake to an enormously long, three-tiered green. All golfers should play this hole once in their lives if only to understand the courage of those Ryder Cup players who have made par or birdie here under monumental pressure.

BELOW *The tough 473-yard (433-m) par-4 18th on the Brabazon Course at the Belfry, one of golf's finest finishing holes, involving two nail-biting crossings of the lake.*

RIGHT *The attractive 10th, a siren hole, luring most golfers into an attempt to drive the green, with the capacity to force most of them to reload – three off the tee!*

CARD OF THE COURSE

Hole	Distance (yards)	Par	Hole	Distance (yards)	Par
1	411	4	10	311	4
2	379	4	11	419	4
3	538	5	12	208	3
4	442	4	13	384	4
5	408	4	14	190	3
6	395	4	15	545	5
7	177	3	16	413	4
8	428	4	17	564	5
9	433	4	18	473	4
Out	3,611	36	In	3,507	36
			Total	7,118	72

N

Ganton

Ganton Golf Club, Scarborough, North Yorkshire, England

If you had to choose a single golf course to encapsulate all that's good about English golf, Ganton would be as good a choice as any. It's old, founded in 1891; it has hosted many high quality tournaments, amateur and professional; it's a mix of heathland and links golf; it's a traditional club yet warmly hospitable; and it's also a great test of all departments of a player's game.

Driving to the course along the busy York–Scarborough road, you could be forgiven for wondering if this were the right road – it just doesn't look like golfing country. Turn down the lane leading to the club and everything changes, even the quality of the air! There are tantalizing glimpses of immaculate fairways and greens, tall pines, cavernous bunkers and hostile gorse. Already it is apparent that only the A game will do.

Ganton is a compact course, which helps to ensure that the pace of play is brisk, although the ingenious routing brings golfers together at different stages of their rounds. Ganton members are sociable, taking every opportunity to compare notes on their respective matches.

INLAND LINKS

What sets the course at Ganton apart from its immediate surroundings is the land on which it was built. This used to be the beach, many thousands of years ago, before the sea retreated to where it is today. Beneath the course is a deep layer of sand giving excellent drainage and supporting the sort of crisp turf more usually encountered at the seaside. Ganton plays like a links, firm and fast. The pitch-and-run shot is usually far more effective than the high-hit wedge, especially in a strong wind, funnelled through the Vale of Pickering.

RIGHT *Ganton's 14th is one of the finest par 4s under 300 yards/274 m in Britain. The setting, in the Vale of Pickering, makes Ganton one of the loveliest places to play.*

▶ Gary Player has said of
Ganton that it is the only inland
course worthy of hosting the
Open Championship – since the
first Open held at Prestwick, the
Open has always been played
on a seaside links.

▶ When Ganton hosted the
1949 Ryder Cup postwar
food rationing was in place.
The American visitors brought
with them 600 steaks, 12
roasting ribs, 12 hams and
12 boxes of bacon. They won!

On the course

The prospect from the 1st tee is inviting, a welcoming fairway rising gently in
front of you, before sliding to the right past bunkers to a green, bunkered on
either side of the entrance. It is not a difficult hole, but you are immediately
aware that sloppy play will not go unpunished. Again, it is the bunkering that
keeps you on your toes on the 2nd, and bunkering provides a stiff challenge for
those aspiring to drive the 3rd green. From here the course twists and turns over
a sequence of delightful holes, meeting the wind from every angle, until on the
14th the course bares its teeth. It may be a short par 4, but it is a brilliant one,
tempting bold play and cruelly punishing the inadequate.

Strong hitting is needed to conquer the 15th, and it will be useful on the
16th tee where you are required to clear a monumental quarry of a bunker
in mid-fairway. The harder task is positioning the drive correctly to grant an
unimpeded approach to the green, raised above bunkers and backed by bright
yellow gorse. The 17th is a brutal long short hole (played as a par 4 by visitors),
and the round ends with a supremely strategic dogleg. Greed will bring disaster!
Then it's time for a drink and a slice of the famous Ganton cake.

CARD OF THE COURSE

Hole	Distance (yards)	Par	Hole	Distance (yards)	Par
1	373	4	10	168	3
2	445	4	11	417	4
3	334	4	12	363	4
4	406	4	13	524	5
5	157	3	14	282	4
6	470	4	15	461	4
7	435	4	16	448	4
8	414	4	17	249	3
9	504	5	18	434	4
Out	3,538	36	In	3,346	35
			Total	6,884	71

Royal Birkdale

Royal Birkdale Golf Club, Southport, Merseyside, England

There is refreshingly little pomp for a club and course with such history. The respect of being chosen for the 100th Open Championship and a consistent ranking in the UK Top 10 are quite sufficient for Royal Birkdale.

A striking sight greets visitors to Royal Birkdale: a white art-deco clubhouse resembling a ship sailing on a tossing sea of sand dunes. It was designed in 1935 to replicate the superstructure of the ocean liners that in those days steamed out from Liverpool in considerable numbers, heading for all corners of the then intact British Empire. Within the clubhouse, however, its creature comforts most definitely belong to the 21st century.

True links golf is played in partnership with nature, and Birkdale's course uses little trickery or human intervention to create its challenges, the difficulties coming instead with subtle design and substantial yardages. Thick rough and willow scrub devour errant shots, and act as a wonderful haven for a wide variety of wildlife. However, the design (evolved over the years by the Hawtree family of golf course architects) is actually very simple: holes weave through valleys between sand hills, creating flat fairways (for a links!)

giving the reward of many yards of roll on a well-struck shot, and a good stance for the next shot. The crests and troughs of that tossing sea of sand dunes are omnipresent, but you are only troubled by them if you stray off line. There are some fine tee and green sites high on them, such as the 11th tee and 12th green.

A long and distinguished championship history

Host to the Open Championship on nine occasions between 1954 and 2008, Royal Birkdale always proves to be an outstanding venue, with its fair nature rewarding good play, while the sand hills lining the fairways create a set of natural grandstands for spectators, the best of any course on the Open roster. The overriding feedback from every Open is that the course is hard but fair, and it is a consistent favourite with the professionals.

▶ The rough can be brutal for Open week. In 1971 Lee Trevino joked: '… at 15 we put down my bag to hunt for a ball, found the ball, lost the bag!'

LEFT *Overlooking the final green, Royal Birkdale's unique clubhouse resembles an ocean liner, so many of which used to steam past the course on their way out from Liverpool.*

A PROUD MOMENT FOR GOLF

One of golf's great gentlemen, Jack Nicklaus generously conceded a short but missable putt to Tony Jacklin on the 18th green at the climax of the 1969 Ryder Cup at Birkdale, a putt that allowed the home team to tie with the Americans. 'I am sure you would have holed, but I was not prepared to see you miss,' was Nicklaus's brotherly remark to his opponent.

The difficult 1st, a long, left-hand dogleg, sets the precedent that accurate hitting is key, with out-of-bounds right, the infamous 'Jutland' bunker on the left, and characteristic mounds that block approaches to the green from poor positions. Although trees are never a factor in regulation play, they often provide a handsome backdrop, such as when they top the dunes behind the 2nd green, a green cunningly contoured and guarded by pot bunkers.

As with all good designs, planning from the tee is essential to allow the correct approach shot to the green, such as on the tough 6th, on which one must flirt with a huge bunker on the right to leave a decent angle to the elevated green. The holes twist and turn through the dunes allowing the prevailing wind to hit from every angle.

There is good variation to the holes, with short par 4s such as the dogleg 5th and downhill 11th both requiring good management. The greens, which were completely rebuilt by Martin Hawtree in the 1990s, are a fine test, with mounds, hollows and clever bunkering around them calling for an imaginative short game, summed up by Seve Ballesteros's famous chip-and-run between the bunkers on the 18th in 1976.

CARD OF THE COURSE

Hole	Distance (yards)	Par
1	449	4
2	421	4
3	407	4
4	203	3
5	344	4
6	480	4
7	177	3
8	457	4
9	411	4
Out	3,349	34
10	403	4
11	408	4
12	183	3
13	498	4
14	198	3
15	544	5
16	416	4
17	547	5
18	472	4
In	3,669	36
Total	7,018	70

Royal Liverpool

Royal Liverpool Golf Club, Hoylake, Wirral, England

Founded in 1869, Royal Liverpool (or Hoylake as it is popularly known) is one of England's oldest golf clubs. Golf was first played here alongside amateur horse and pony races, for this was the site of the Liverpool Hunt Club. Naturally, the horses were not expected to charge up and down the sand dunes, so, for the most part, this is an unusually flat course. But appearances can be deceptive, especially here.

In no time at all (1872) Hoylake had attracted its first professional tournament – in fact the first of any significance outside Scotland. The first prize was almost double the prize for the Open Championship. It attracted a small but distinguished field with Young Tom Morris emerging victorious. Next up was the inaugural Amateur Championship (1885), followed by its first Open Championship (1897). The winner on this occasion was Royal Liverpool's own Harold Hilton; he and his club companion John Ball were the only amateurs to win the Open Championship until the emergence of Bobby Jones, who won at Hoylake in 1930. This was to become the second leg of his incredible 'Impregnable Quadrilateral', when he won the Open and Amateur Championships of the United States and Britain in the same year. The Open returned to Hoylake several times, but after Roberto de Vicenzo's victory in 1967 there was a lengthy gap until 2006, when Tiger Woods showed everybody else how to play the course.

RIGHT *The 12th green presents a difficult target, raised up on top of the dunes, but it gives wonderful views over the Dee Estuary to the Flintshire hills.*

Woods – the great strategist

As he had done previously at St Andrews in 2005, Woods analysed the course from the point of view of his own strengths, deciding that it was too dangerous to use the driver prospectively from the tee. He reckoned that if he played for position rather than length, making sure that his tee shot landed in the best spot from which to approach the green, his long-iron play to the green would get him close to the hole. His approach play that week was imperious.

The order of the holes was altered for the Open, but more usually Hoylake begins with a unique hole, a bunkerless par 4 on which it is possible to drive out of bounds on either side. The green adjoins a 'cop' (a grassy bank, typical of Hoylake) which is also out of bounds. Like the first hole, most of the early holes are level, but there is a relentlessness about the probing that never lets up. The wind rarely lets up either.

As the round progresses the character of the course changes gradually until the 8th, when the pitch is made steeply uphill to a rolling green standing on top of the dunes, giving way to a glorious sequence of seaside holes with expansive views. The pick of these must be the 12th, a majestic par 4 beginning with a drive to a low, curving fairway, followed by a long second shot uphill to a brilliantly sited green, repelling all but the finest approaches. Woods solved its problems on the second day of the Open by pitching in for an eagle. His approach, stone dead, on the final afternoon was breathtaking. Great golf on a great course!

▶ For the 2006 Open Championship a number of alterations were made to the course, including a brand new 17th hole (played as the 1st for the championship). The old green was so near to a road that it was not unknown for players to putt out of bounds.

CARD OF THE COURSE

Hole	Distance (yards)	Par
1	429	4
2	372	4
3	528	5
4	202	3
5	453	4
6	423	4
7	198	3
8	534	5
9	393	4
Out	3,532	36
10	448	4
11	198	3
12	456	4
13	161	3
14	554	5
15	459	4
16	560	5
17	454	4
18	436	4
In	3,726	36
Total	7,258	72

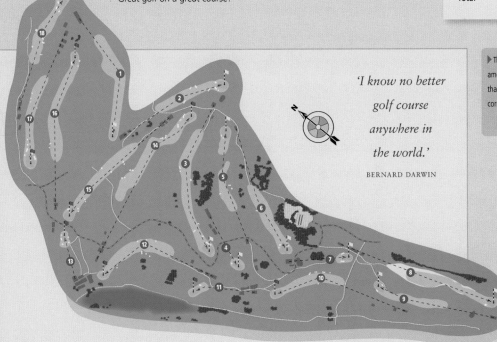

'I know no better golf course anywhere in the world.'

BERNARD DARWIN

▶ The 6th hole is unusual among championship courses in that the drive is made over the corner of an orchard.

Wentworth

Wentworth

West Course, Wentworth Club, Virginia Water, Surrey, England

Driving through the vast Wentworth Estate is a voyage of discovery. The mansions of the rich and famous line the lanes and drives, many of them backing on to the fairways of the three golf courses that occasionally cross the roads, causing the driver to stop while a four-ball launches its tee shots on their journeys.

ABOVE *Wentworth's West Course is as visually attractive as it is demanding. It is one of those courses that invites you to play good shots. This is the par-3 2nd.*

The Wentworth Estate came into being in the 1920s through the vision, entrepreneurial skills and extraordinary confidence of a developer – George Tarrant. When it came to constructing the golf courses, Tarrant knew exactly who to use – Harry Colt. Colt and Tarrant had collaborated on a similar scheme some years earlier at St George's Hill, and the success of both ventures has ensured that both are among the most desirable places to live in the whole London area.

Colt built the East Course in 1924. Today it measures only a little over 6,000 yards/5,486 m, but it is a thoroughly entertaining course and was good enough to host a match between the professionals of America and Great Britain and Ireland in 1926, thus paving the way for the Ryder Cup. The East was also the venue for the inaugural Curtis Cup, between women amateur golfers of the United States and Great Britain and Ireland, in 1932. Second up was the West Course, also Colt-designed, of 1926. There was then a gap of over 60 years until the third course, the Edinburgh, opened in 1990. This was designed by John Jacobs in association with Gary Player and Bernard Gallagher.

The Burma Road

When it opened, the West Course was found to be long and hard, tough enough for it to be dubbed the Burma Road. Its length is not so fearsome today but the name has stuck and twice a year television audiences get to see it in fine condition, hosting the PGA Championship in the spring and the World Matchplay in the autumn. Recent adjustments to the course by Ernie Els (who lives on the estate) have pushed the overall length up from just over 7,000 yards/6,400 m to more than 7,300 yards/6,675 m. Visitors playing it from the yellow tees still find it quite long enough at over 6,700 yards/6,125 m.

Length is not everything, however, and some of the best holes are modest on paper. The delightful 154-yard/141-m 2nd, for instance, is played from a high tee across a road to an elusive ledge green. The 6th, 7th and 8th are each among the shorter par 4s, but their greens are notoriously hard to locate. The short 14th is played uphill to a multi-level green, the hill being steep enough to deceive the eye, and club selection further complicated if there is a wind. Similarly, the 16th regularly sets problems for the professionals under tournament conditions.

A new tee has been found for the 17th, stretching it to a monstrous – and treacherous – 610 yards/558 m. It is all too easy to drive out of bounds on the left, so the natural reaction is to err to the right, increasing the length of the hole and very probably resulting in a clinging lie, or even finishing behind a tree. Nor is the green easy to find, on high ground, the fairway constantly curving. The Els-modified 18th is now a particularly strong finishing hole.

▶ In addition to the PGA Championship and World Matchplay, the West Course has hosted the Ryder Cup (1953) and the Canada Cup (1956), when Ben Hogan made one of his all-too-rare visits to the UK, winning the tournament with Sam Snead as partner.

CARD OF THE COURSE

Hole	Distance (yards)	Par
1	473	5
2	154	3
3	465	4
4	552	5
5	212	3
6	418	4
7	396	4
8	401	4
9	452	4
Out	3,523	36
10	184	3
11	416	4
12	531	5
13	470	4
14	179	3
15	490	4
16	383	4
17	610	5
18	538	5
In	3,801	37
Total	7,324	73

Woodhall Spa

Hotchkin Course, Woodhall Spa, Lincolnshire, England

Of all Britain's great courses the Hotchkin Course at Woodhall Spa must be the least known – for the very simple reason that it lies in a remote corner of the country, not really on the way to or from anywhere. Despite its inviting title, Woodhall Spa is little more than a charming village, but it has had a golf course since 1890.

The club had rather a troubled history, and the local landowner, Stafford Vere Hotchkin, repeatedly came to the rescue, first by writing off the club's rent arrears and in 1919 by buying the club. After a succession of moves and different course layouts, the club was lucky enough to possess, by this time, a fine Harry Colt course laid out on a rare tract of sandy heath. But Hotchkin was not merely a financial benefactor, he was also a more than competent golfer and a course designer himself. Between 1919 and his death in 1953 he

made a large number of refinements to the design, turning the course into one of England's most demanding. Hotchkin's son Neil continued to run the club after his father's death, which ensured that the design was not tampered with and Hotchkin's ethos maintained. In 1995 he sold the course to the English Golf Union (EGU), who made their headquarters there, bringing in Donald Steel to build a second – and utterly different – course (the Bracken), while keeping Hotchkin's course in the manner of which he would have approved.

RIGHT *The bunkering at Woodhall Spa is among the most formidable in Britain. It is deep, steep-faced and prolific. This is the 5th green, surrounded by sand.*

▶ During a club match in 1982 a member holed the 12th in one – as, then, did his opponent, for the half!

▶ One of Hotchkin's principles of golf course design was: 'The best results are obtained by making a course conform to the natural surroundings that already exist, so that it will not look artificial and fail to blend with the landscape.' Woodhall Spa is a shining example.

▶ Because of its location Woodhall Spa has staged few professional tournaments, but it has featured prominently in the amateur calendar, hosting such tournaments as the English Amateur, Brabazon Trophy, St Andrews Trophy and Ladies' British Open Amateur.

CARD OF THE COURSE

Hole	Distance (yards)	Par	Hole	Distance (yards)	Par
1	361	4	10	338	4
2	442	4	11	437	4
3	415	4	12	172	3
4	414	4	13	451	4
5	148	3	14	521	5
6	526	5	15	321	4
7	470	4	16	395	4
8	209	3	17	336	4
9	584	5	18	540	5
Out	3,569	36	In	3,511	37
			Total	7,080	73

England's most frightening bunkers?

Until you have played Woodhall Spa it is difficult to imagine just how ferocious its bunkers are. It is a moot point whether Ganton or Woodhall Spa has the most savage bunkering in England. Ganton's are more visible and perhaps more frightening to the eye. Woodhall Spa's bunkers are deeper – sinister trenches very often topped off with eyebrows of heather – and sometimes invisible from a distance. A bunker may be as deep as the height of a man. In some cases these are set tight against elevated greens and you may have to raise the ball 10 feet/ 3 m vertically to gain the safety of the putting surface. The strange thing is that Ganton and Woodhall Spa are such lovely courses that, however roughly they may treat you, you still enjoy the experience immensely.

Woodhall Spa charms you from the outset, with a delicate, short two-shot hole to get play under way. You could be lulled into a false sense of security, but on the 2nd hole the course bares its teeth, with the deepest of bunkers threatening the drive of all lengths of hitters, and the green has a narrow entrance. And if a bunker does not get you the heather most surely will. It may look lovely, but a rash shot out of it may result in a broken wrist.

What makes Woodhall Spa so enticing is the wonderful variety of the holes, with no two the same. There are great long two-shotters, but it may be the collection of par 3s (only three of them) that remain in the memory longest.

Celtic Manor

Twenty Ten Course, Celtic Manor Resort, Newport, Wales

The golf courses at Celtic Manor, host to the Ryder Cup in 2010, are contemporary in every way, but the ground over which they run is steeped in ancient history. They overlook the remains of the Roman town of Caerleon and, running from it, the Via Julia was an important communication route connecting this Welsh outpost to the Roman settlements in England. Its remains cross the Celtic Manor estate.

In the 5th century the lands were acquired by the Bishops of Llandaff and in the 17th century a manor house was built for the local high sheriff. But the estate as it now is first took shape in the 1860s when the enormously prosperous industrialist, Thomas Powell, had Coldra House built for his son. Subsequently the house became a maternity hospital. It closed in 1975 and was in danger of falling into ruin until a wealthy businessman, Sir Terry Matthews, bought it in 1981, restoring it for use initially as a small luxury hotel. Since then the story has been one of considerable expansion. The hotel can now accommodate almost 2,000 conference delegates and in 1995 golf arrived on the scene in the shape of the Roman Road Course, which, as its name suggests, keeps close company with the Via Julia.

The Roman Road Course was designed by one of the legends of golf course design, Robert Trent Jones, who in his 70-year career built over 300 courses, including the Ryder Cup venue, Valderrama, in Spain, and made alterations to a further 150. Jones returned to Celtic Manor to build a short course, Coldra Woods, and later to team up with his son, Robert Jr, to lay out the enormously long Wentwood Hills Course – an extraordinary mix of alpine holes and others that might have been lifted bodily from Florida, with the obligatory lakes to the fore in the lowland section.

Bold decisions

Matthews was ambitious for his resort. He wanted to attract the biggest stars in the game to play there and he set out to bring the Ryder Cup to Wales for the first time. His problem was that none of his existing courses could accommodate such a tournament. Roman Road was not tough enough and Wentwood Hills was spectator-unfriendly, with an exhausting hill climb required on the back nine. Drastic measures were needed, and Matthews was not afraid to take bold decisions.

The boldest decision was to abandon the Wentwood Hills Course, considered the jewel in the crown of the resort. It has not been wasted, for the upland holes have been incorporated in a new course designed by Colin Montgomerie, and nine of the low-lying holes have been retained as part of the course specifically designed to attract the Ryder Cup, lying entirely in the Usk Valley. Matthews's brave move was successful, and the Ryder Cup matches will be played in Wales for the first time in 2010, on this course now known as the Twenty Ten.

As might be expected, it is a heroic course playing to almost 7,500 yards/6,858 m from the back tees. For those matches that make it to the par-5 18th hole – one of three par 5s over 600 yards/(549 m – there remains a death-or-glory gamble on whether to try to reach the green in two across a green-front lake. Roman gladiators would have understood the pressures; Ryder Cup spectators will relish the contest.

▶ Thomas Powell, founder of the Powell-Duffryn Company and the world's first millionaire, employed 13,500 workers in his coal business, 11,600 of them working underground.

LEFT *The tranquillity of the Usk Valley will become a cauldron of high emotion when the Ryder Cup matches are played at Celtic Manor. This is the 14th.*

CARD OF THE COURSE

Hole	Distance (yards)	Par
1	465	4
2	610	5
3	189	3
4	461	4
5	457	4
6	452	4
7	213	3
8	439	4
9	666	5
Out	3,952	36
10	210	3
11	562	5
12	458	4
13	189	3
14	413	4
15	377	4
16	508	4
17	211	3
18	613	5
In	3,541	35
Total	7,493	71

'There's water, drivable par 4s and the finishing stretch is fantastic.'

IAN WOOSNAM,
CAPTAIN OF EUROPEAN TEAM,
2006 RYDER CUP

Royal County Down

Royal County Down Golf Club, Newcastle, County Down, Northern Ireland

On the coast of Dundrum Bay, backed by the Mourne Mountains, 18 holes weave purposefully through dunes and gorse to create, in the words of Tom Watson, 'a pure links'. For over 100 years, Old Tom Morris's routing has changed little, and as such there is a sense that the course has always been here, quietly tucked away in this beautifully unassuming place.

Don't be mistaken in assuming that the age and tradition of the course have left it obsolete in today's game. Though quite capable of hosting major tournaments, Royal County Down has opted to avoid these events, fearing that the course and indigenous wildlife would suffer from trampling spectators and media villages – the Senior British Open and Walker Cup are the biggest events of recent times. It is especially impressive, therefore, that many great players have made the pilgrimage to this wonderful course simply to experience it. Famously, Tiger Woods has chosen these holes to sharpen his links skills before an Open Championship.

A perfect nine?

The front nine is commonly regarded as the best front nine in golf (not to say that the back nine is shabby). A great starting hole, the par-5 1st is reachable in two, but one must carry the ball long down the left-hand side to take advantage of the sloping fairway, which bounds the ball forwards towards the green. As poor drives are punished, with dunes on both sides and the beach on the right, this hole sets the precedent that control is a necessity. Another somewhat daunting feature during the round is that of playing tee shots over dunes, blind or semi-blind.

After the first couple of drives, which play in the same direction over intimidating hills, when guests reach the 4th tee members often allow them to set up with driver aiming over the dune before pointing out that this is a par 3 played in the opposite direction! Looking in the correct direction from this elevated tee, one is blessed by a gorgeous view of the mountains and sea, but the player can also see the countless challenges ahead. After a carry over gorse bushes, nine brutish bunkers surround a green with large drop-offs to both sides and the back.

Possibly the best hole on the back nine is the 13th. Bunkers plague the dogleg on the right-hand side, and a decent hit down the left is rewarded with lengthy run on the mounds of the firm fairway. If the drive is too short, sight of the green is blocked by the gorse-banked dune on the dogleg. The broad, sloping green is nestled among dunes to create its own amphitheatre, backed by swathes of lilac heather. The strength of holes like this, coupled with picturesque scenery and legendary hospitality, have led Royal County Down to a consistent ranking as one of the world's Top 10 courses.

LEFT *Slieve Donard, the highest of the Mourne Mountains, overlooks Dundrum Bay and the historic Royal County Down links. This is the excellent 3rd hole, viewed from behind the green.*

▶ In 1933, in the Irish Open Amateur Championship, Eric Fiddian recorded two holes-in-one in the final, yet still lost.

CARD OF THE COURSE

Hole	Distance (yards)	Par
1	539	5
2	444	4
3	477	4
4	213	3
5	440	4
6	398	4
7	145	3
8	430	4
9	486	4
Out	3,572	35
10	197	3
11	440	4
12	527	5
13	444	4
14	212	3
15	467	4
16	337	4
17	435	4
18	550	5
In	3,609	36
Total	7,181	71

BELOW *The bunkers at Royal County Down are serious, both in expanse and depth. Many are topped off by eyebrows of heather or clinging rough grass. These threaten the drive at the 8th.*

'For visual splendour and golf on a heroic scale, there is nothing better.'

DONALD STEEL, *CLASSIC GOLF LINKS OF GREAT BRITAIN AND IRELAND*

Ballybunion

Ballybunion

The Old Course, Ballybunion, County Kerry, Republic of Ireland

A round of golf on the Old Course at Ballybunion is a unique experience. None other than Tom Watson would agree. He was very much responsible for alerting the world to the existence of this extraordinary place, which was largely unknown outside Ireland when he first visited in 1981. Now acknowledged as one of the world's greatest courses, many a star golfer has made the pilgrimage to play it.

Ballybunion is a long-established club, founded in 1893 in the far west of Ireland on a stretch of quite incomparable dunes overlooking the Atlantic Ocean. There are many golf courses in the west of Ireland set on dunes overlooking the Atlantic, but what sets Ballybunion apart is the way the course is routed over, through, across and along the dunes. So the golfer is asked to play a huge catalogue of different shots throughout the round to adapt to the constantly changing topography.

BELOW *The full might, majesty, dominion and power of Ballybunion as portrayed by the conjunction of the wonderfully sited 10th green and beyond it the magical 11th fairway.*

COASTAL EROSION

It is the stuff of nightmares – seeing your course washed away by the unstoppable power of the sea. The venerable Olympic Club in San Francisco lost a number of holes to the Pacific Ocean some years ago. Ballybunion, too, faced the prospect of losing some of its finest holes to the Atlantic Ocean in the 1970s. An appeal was launched, and that was when Ballybunion found that it had friends, generous ones, all over the world. With the threat of global warming raising sea levels erosion is on many clubs' agendas throughout the world.

Natural hazards

The Old Course excites golfers of all abilities. The round starts ominously, for there is a graveyard awaiting the merest slice from the 1st tee, and from here to the corner of the dogleg on the 6th the course slides into gear rather as an Irish morning slowly gathers momentum. At this point the adrenaline kicks in, with a delicious pitch up to a green on top of the dunes, the first of a series of greens that seriously tests every department of the approach game. This hole has no need of a bunker and, once away from the opening (inland) holes, there are remarkably few bunkers on the course as a whole. Such is the brilliance of the green sites that grassy swales and fall-aways protect the holes even more strongly than sand would.

Indeed, one of the finest holes on the course – one of the world's great holes – has no bunker, either. It is the unforgettable 11th, a gorgeous hole tumbling down through the sand hills alongside the Atlantic with a green cleverly defended by encircling dunes. There are great holes still to come, but it was the short 8th that particularly appealed to Watson on his first visit, with an all-or-nothing shot to a tiny green and desperate recovery work required should the tee shot fail to hold the putting surface.

Ballybunion boasts back-to-back par 3s on the inward half, the 14th and 15th. Like every hole here, they were dictated naturally by the exciting land forms, and the 15th is a great short hole, played to a marvellous green backed by the Atlantic Ocean. Then the excellent 16th and 17th both make excursions to the oceanside. Ballybunion should be on every golfer's must-play list.

▶ Ballybunion was enlarged into an 18-hole course in 1926. The 'designer' was a Mr Smyth. His layout was so good that when Tom Simpson was engaged to upgrade it in 1937 he suggested only three minor changes.

▶ Ballybunion is so far from any major population centre that it has hosted the Irish Open only once, in 2000. Sweden's Patrik Sjöland emerged victorious after opening rounds of 64 and 65.

CARD OF THE COURSE

Hole	Distance (yards)	Par
1	392	4
2	445	4
3	220	3
4	498	5
5	508	5
6	364	4
7	423	4
8	153	3
9	454	4
Out	3,457	36
10	359	4
11	449	4
12	192	3
13	484	5
14	131	3
15	216	3
16	490	5
17	385	4
18	379	4
In	3,085	35
Total	6,542	71

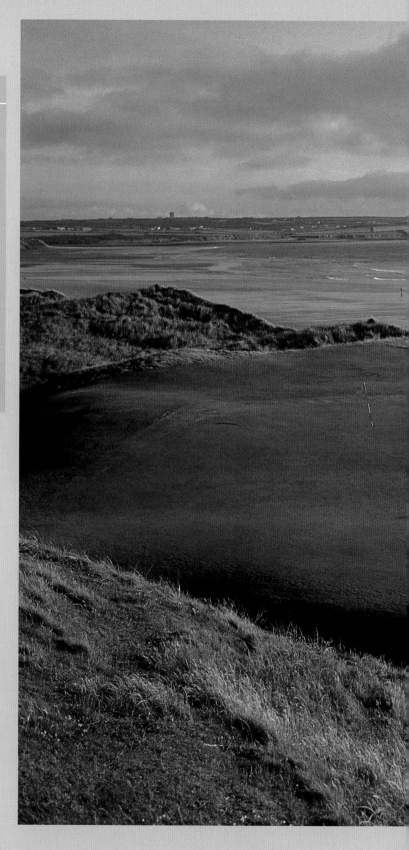

FINEST PIECE OF LINKSLAND

In the late 1960s the decision was taken to purchase further duneland to the south of the existing links. By 1980 sufficient funds had been raised to consider building a second course and Robert Trent Jones was approached. He wrote, 'I was given both a once-in-a-lifetime opportunity and a terrifying challenge . . . the property I had to work with is perhaps the finest piece of linksland in the world.' In 1984 the Cashen Course was completed but it is proving to be controversial. Jones made spectacular use of the site, but the course is too hard for higher-handicap players. That said, the Cashen possesses a fabulous collection of green sites and Ballybunion as a whole offers a wonderful test of approach work.

RIGHT *Tom Watson rated the 11th as 'one of the toughest holes in the world . . . a small target with not a lot of room to miss right or left.'*

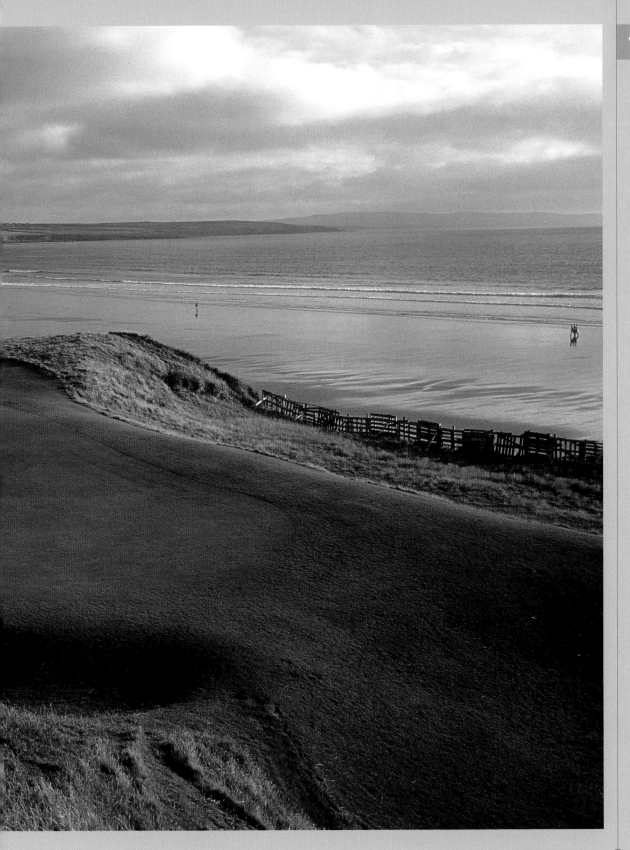

Augusta

Augusta National Golf Club, Georgia, USA

Tennis at Wimbledon or Flushing Meadow, motor racing at Le Mans or Indianapolis, racing at Longchamp or Churchill Downs, golf at St Andrews or . . .? Most people, even those who have little knowledge of golf, would probably answer, 'Augusta National'. Its modern-day fame comes from its hosting of the Masters, the first major of the professional golfing year, and the only major held annually on the same course. But that fame would not have arisen had it not been for one Robert Tyre Jones, or Bobby or Bob, depending on which side of the Atlantic you come from.

Jones was the greatest amateur golfer of all time, winning five US Amateur titles and one Amateur Championship in Britain. But he was also good enough to take on and beat the best professionals of the day (the 1920s) taking the US Open on four occasions and the British Open on three. Having won the Amateur and Open Championships of America and Britain in the same year, 1930, he retired from competitive golf, much to the relief of the rest of them!

BELOW *Catch your drive perfectly and you can take advantage of this downslope to reduce the playing length of the 10th hole significantly. The raised green is not one to miss.*

Jones's unlikely design partner

When Jones came to establish his ideal golf course, on which he and his wealthy friends might play, he had some novel ideas about how it might be set up, making the best players feel seriously tested while somehow allowing the high-handicapper to get round in 100 or so without feeling like abandoning golf for good. And it was a pure accident that led Jones to find the ideal architect to help him realize this concept. In 1929 Jones had been knocked out of the US Amateur Championship unexpectedly early. That year the event was held at Pebble Beach, California, so he took the

CARD OF THE COURSE

Hole	Distance (yards)	Par
1	435	4
2	575	5
3	350	4
4	205	3
5	455	4
6	180	3
7	410	4
8	570	5
9	460	4
Out	3,640	36
10	495	4
11	490	4
12	155	3
13	510	5
14	440	4
15	500	5
16	170	3
17	425	4
18	465	4
In	3,650	36
Total	7,290	72

opportunity to play nearby Cypress Point and Pasatiempo, courses designed by Alister MacKenzie, a Leeds physician turned golf course architect – one of the very best in the world in fact. Jones knew immediately that he had found the right man for the job.

Although today's course is little altered from the original (a new 16th hole and revisions to the bunkering) it is set up for the Masters in a manner far removed from what Jones or MacKenzie could have anticipated. Quite simply, the greens are maintained at frighteningly fast speeds, and trees and rough have been planted where previously there were neither. It provides a spectacle for television and it prevents scores becoming ridiculously low, but no high-handicapper would survive a hole, let alone 18!

Yet it remains a fabulous (and fabulously beautiful) course. How often we viewers are on tenterhooks as the leaders pass through the treacherous Amen Corner (11th, 12th and 13th holes) with Rae's Creek awaiting just the tiniest slip up. Will they risk all and try to get on the 13th and 15th greens in two? And there are – to us – impossible putts on the 16th and 17th greens. Or how about that slick, downhill 8-footer on the last green that must go in or we are into a play-off? The Masters is always dramatic.

▶ Augusta is ablaze with azaleas during the Masters. Before it was a golf course, this was a nursery, Fruitlands, owned by a Belgian horticulturalist, Baron Berckmans, who popularized the azalea in America.

▶ When Tiger Woods won the 2001 Masters he became the first player to hold all four majors at the same time (having won the US Open, Open Championship and USPGA the previous year). He was 65 under par for the four tournaments.

Augusta

A COVETED INVITATION

The Masters is unique among the majors for having an invited field of under 100 competitors of whom a number will be amateurs. The spectators, too, are a select group, tickets being guarded jealously by those lucky enough to have them, for they are not available for public sale, and any spectator behaving in an inappropriate or unsporting manner will have their ticket confiscated in what is effectively a life ban. Consequently the same patrons return year after year, their collective experience adding to their generous support for every player, giving the Masters' galleries a deserved reputation for knowledgeable and considerate support. In this, of course, they are upholding the traditions for sportsmanship embodied by Bob Jones.

The 13th (below), 16th (main picture) and 12th (top right) are favourite holes with Masters' spectators, for each hole witnesses great drama every day: an unlikely birdie or eagle, perhaps, or an undesired skirmish with the water and a rapid tumble down the leader board.

Kiawah Island

Kiawah Island

Ocean Course, Kiawah Island Golf Resort, South Carolina, USA

Never has a name rung so true as 'The Ocean Course', for the Atlantic Ocean is in view on every single hole. Ten holes are directly on the coast, the greatest number of seaside holes on any course in the northern hemisphere, and the other eight play parallel to them. This remarkable feature not only provides some of the most scenic golf imaginable, but also makes the course massively affected by the wind. Interestingly, as with the 17th at Sawgrass, this trademark was not intended by the designer Pete Dye, who had planned to sit the course behind the dunes until his wife Alice suggested raising the course in order to provide the stunning sea views.

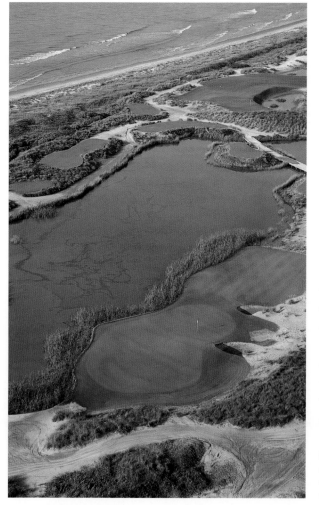

The unbelievable beauty of the course disguises its brutal difficulty. Dye made use of the natural environment, with dunes and tall grasses devouring poor shots. The most distinctive design feature is that different shot options are always available. Many holes reward daring carries, but players are never forced to take these lines. From the tee and fairway, players must pick a shot to suit their ability and the conditions.

The wide range of options makes for innovative golf, and it is also mandatory on a course so affected by the wind. It has been estimated that wind changes can alter club selection by up to eight clubs, so there needs to be a route for every strength and direction of wind.

Extensive lakes and vast tracts of sandy waste await the inaccurate shot, making this a fine matchplay course but the very devil on which to keep a medal card going.

LEFT *Like the 17th at Sawgrass, Dye wondered if the par-3 17th was dramatic enough, so he added an enormous lake to carry!*

RIGHT *The sand areas are not considered hazards so you may ground your club. This is the par-4 9th hole.*

'The biggest diabolical thing on the whole golf course.'

PETE DYE'S DESCRIPTION OF THE 2ND HOLE

N

Creative challenges

The par-5 2nd hole is a good reflection of the course. From the tee, players will be struck by the epic view towards the ocean. But they will also be faced with golfing dilemmas in choosing the correct angle from the tee to cross the marshland that spells golfing disaster if you come up short. A safe shot plays out right for the less bold. If the drive was overly cautious, the second shot must be laid up short of another marsh, 110 yards/101 m in front of the green. Good players should be able to get around the green in two, but that is not the end of the story, as the green is a difficult raised shelf, rolling away into a deep bunker. After a gentle opening hole, the 2nd can be a real nemesis, and even the professionals rack up big scores here. In the 1991 Ryder Cup, Seve Ballesteros won the 2nd with a double-bogey to Wayne Levi's 8!

Like a true links, the options for shot-making are endless, and the longer holes tend to offer a route in on the ground, as well as an airborne approach. You are continually challenged to think hard and pick the right shot. With the design so demanding of creative golf it is no surprise that the Ryder Cup was such a success – the PGA Championship in 2012 should be a real treat.

CARD OF THE COURSE

Hole	Distance (yards)	Par	Hole	Distance (yards)	Par
1	395	4	10	439	4
2	543	5	11	562	5
3	390	4	12	466	4
4	453	4	13	404	4
5	207	3	14	194	3
6	455	4	15	421	4
7	527	5	16	579	5
8	197	3	17	221	3
9	464	4	18	439	4
Out	3,631	36	In	3,725	36
			Total	7,356	72

Pebble Beach

Pebble Beach Golf Links, Pebble Beach, California, USA

Pebble Beach is universally regarded as one of the world's best public courses. It was chosen as the venue for the 100th US Open in 2000, the fourth time it had hosted the US Open, yet anybody can simply book a tee time and play on this historic stage. There are, of course, two snags: it is very expensive and you must book long in advance.

Pebble Beach opened in 1919 and ten years later became the first course west of the Mississippi to host the US Amateur Championship. A young Jack Nicklaus capped an impressive amateur career here when he won the 1961 US Amateur. The 'Golden Bear' was again victorious when Pebble Beach staged its first US Open in 1972. Despite coming second to Tom Watson in 1982, his affection for Pebble Beach never waned, and eventually he bade farewell to the US Open here in 2000, an emotional Nicklaus poignantly sitting on the fence behind the 18th tee, surveying one of the best finishing holes in golf.

The par-5 18th requires nerves of steel as the entire hole teeters on the edge of the Pacific. It really should be played as a three-shot hole, often with a 3-wood from the tee. In the 2000 US Open, even the apparently infallible Tiger Woods, who would coast to victory by a margin of 15 shots, managed to pull his tee shot into the sea.

Tom Watson showed the perfect way to play the closing holes at Pebble Beach in the 1982 US Open. With one of golf's most famous chip-ins, he made birdie from the rough on the par-3 17th to claim a one-shot lead over Nicklaus. Sensibly Watson hit a 3-wood for position from the 18th tee and laid up with his second shot in the fairway with a 7-iron to leave himself a short iron approach. Again he played safely, approaching the heart of the green as the pin was tucked in behind the front bunker. From there he finished in style, rolling the 20-ft/6-m putt into the centre of the cup for a birdie, birdie finish.

Glorious coastal holes

Stunning holes are abundant here, and from the 4th there are seven consecutive oceanside holes, including the amazing 7th – with wind blowing into your face and the ocean awaiting if you overhit your shot, the prospect from the tee is nerve-racking (*see* photograph page 59). The sequence from the 8th to the 10th is one of the greatest trios of consecutive par 4s in world golf. At the 8th, after an exciting drive, you play an awesome approach shot across a corner of the ocean to find the typically small and unreceptive green.

Throughout the round you are presented with daunting drives at undulating fairways, but it is the approach shots where ingenuity is called for. On one hole with wind behind, only a high fade will stop on the tiny green, but on the next you may be playing straight into the wind and having to hit a low punch shot. With a course designed for such inventive golf, and backed by breathtaking views, many golfers would share Jack Nicklaus's view that this is possibly the best course in the world. As Billy Andrade once said, 'It's the Holy Grail for us.'

▶ In 2001 *Golf Digest* ranked Pebble Beach the No.1 course in America , the first time a public course achieved this position. It's a course that everyone wants to play, and it will cost you around $500 to do so.

▶ 17-Mile Drive, which passes through Pebble Beach, is a private toll road. The Pebble Beach Company owns the copyright on all photographic sites on this scenic route – and there are a lot of them!

LEFT *One of the best-known, and most photographed, closing holes in golf, the 18th at Pebble Beach, hugging the Pacific Ocean for every one of its 543 yards/497 m.*

CARD OF THE COURSE

Hole	Distance (yards)	Par
1	381	4
2	502	5
3	390	4
4	331	4
5	188	3
6	513	5
7	106	3
8	418	4
9	466	4
Out	3,295	36
10	446	4
11	380	4
12	202	3
13	399	4
14	573	5
15	397	4
16	403	4
17	178	3
18	543	5
In	3,521	36
Total	6,816	72

'I've loved this course from the first time I saw it. It's possibly the best in the world.'

JACK NICKLAUS

Pine Valley

Pine Valley Golf Club, Clementon, New Jersey, USA

Pine Valley has a reputation for being the hardest course in the world. Yes, the Ocean Course at Kiawah Island might play considerably harder from the back tees in a gale, and many a modern layout, with water on all 18 holes, could be tricked up to be almost unplayable. But, on a daily basis, Pine Valley is the hardest simply because it asks the golfer to play total golf on every single shot, with the penalty for failure dire. What is so extraordinary about Pine Valley is that no one who has played it would begrudge it a single dropped stroke. It is a masterpiece.

It was a Pittsburgh hotelier, George Crump, a fine amateur player in his own right, who came up with the idea for this course. He had clear views about what he wanted to achieve and for some five years he lived on the site, directing construction. However, he was wise enough to consult others, including Walter Travis and Jerome Travers, two of America's leading amateur golfers in the early years of the 20th century, and the English architect Harry Colt. Quite how much each of them contributed may never be known, but Crump died in 1918 before the course was finished. Today's 12th to 15th holes were completed by Hugh Wilson, the genius of Merion, probably with advice and input from Hugh Alison, Colt's design partner.

Pine Valley today is rather different from the course that was completed in 1919, in that hundreds of thousands of trees have matured to add to the existing perils. Essentially there are tees, narrow strips of grass, which might be called fairways, swathes of sandy waste and a dense forest – and fiendish greens.

BELOW *The shortest hole at Pine Valley, the 10th, is a wicked little hole. The target is tiny, and missing it is likely to call for miraculous powers of recovery.*

BELOW The 5th hole remains extraordinarily demanding with 21st-century clubs and balls. What it must have been like with those of 1919 hardly bears thinking about.

The ultimate in punitive golf

There are no weak holes at Pine Valley, but three in particular have world renown – the 5th, 7th and 13th. The 5th is a brutal 'short' hole – a full carry of around 230 yards/210 m over a lake and up a hill to a raised green isolated in the woodlands. It would be intimidating at half its length.

Most famous of all the holes is the 7th, a remarkable par 5 made infamous by Hell's Half Acre, a huge expanse of sand splitting the fairway between 285 yards/261 m and 385 yards/352 m from the tee. Get your drive wrong and you cannot clear it with your second. Get the drive right but mishit the second and you are still facing disaster. Get your first and second right and you are left with a devilish pitch to a green entirely surrounded by sand.

It is something similar on the 13th. You drive over a wilderness to an island fairway in the far distance. Then follows a terrifying shot, all carry, of 200 yards/183 m or more over scrub and sand to a green angled away to the left with no margin for error front, back, left or right. Yet despite the difficulties of each hole there is amazing variety to the course, with welcome change of pace, particularly within the two-shot holes. Hard yes, but still we come back for more.

CARD OF THE COURSE

Hole	Distance (yards)	Par
1	421	4
2	368	4
3	198	3
4	451	4
5	235	3
6	387	4
7	636	5
8	326	4
9	459	4
Out	3,481	35
10	161	3
11	397	4
12	337	4
13	486	4
14	220	3
15	615	5
16	475	4
17	345	4
18	483	4
In	3,519	35
Total	7,000	70

TPC Sawgrass

Stadium Course, TPC Sawgrass, Ponte Vedra Beach, Florida, USA

When the two-year-old course hosted its first tournament, the Players Championship of 1982, the professionals were almost unanimous in their verdict: they hated it! Although the design had always aimed to be tough, clearly it was too much, and Pete Dye, the renowned US golf course designer, modified the course slightly to soften the greens and change particularly brutal bunkers. The changes worked and the Players Championship has now become the unofficial fifth major.

The professionals' opinions were especially important at Sawgrass as TPC (Tournament Players Club) courses are owned by the PGA (Professional Golfers' Association) for the purpose of hosting tournaments. The course is respected by the professionals as the clever design does not favour a specific type of player. Long hitters like Davis Love and Tiger Woods have won the Players Championship, but so have those relying on accuracy such as Hal Sutton, Justin Leonard and Tom Kite. Adam Scott won at the age of 23; the following year Fred Funk won aged 48.

The island green

The PGA ownership is reflected in the design, in that the course was created for tournament golf. Huge amounts of earth were removed from the site and used to create spectator mounds surrounding the fairways and greens, the deep holes left from excavation being filled with water, creating plentiful lakes. Such is the fame of the island-green 17th, one of golf's most feared short holes, that an American sports channel devotes itself to showing uninterrupted coverage of the hole during the Players Championship. Interestingly, Dye never intended the 17th green to be surrounded by water. He was planning to make it a giant bunker until his wife suggested the island.

Water comes into play on most holes, notably on the brutal 18th. With a lake on the left of this tough dogleg, players are faced with a 'bite off as much as you can chew' concept from the tee. If the drive is not perfectly placed you must lay up the approach, as an aggressive second shot, especially from the clingy rough, tends to be water bound.

'We have seventeen pretty good holes at the TPC and one bad one – the 17th.'

TOM KITE

▸ The weight of the Spanish tiles on the roof of the Mediterranean-style clubhouse is equivalent to two jumbo jets.

▸ It is estimated that over 100,000 balls are scooped out of the water on the 17th hole every year.

LEFT *The hole they all copy: the 18th at TPC Sawgrass, with its invitation to bite off as much as you dare with 40,000 spectators watching you.*

CARD OF THE COURSE

Hole	Distance (yards)	Par	Hole	Distance (yards)	Par
1	392	4	10	424	4
2	532	5	11	535	5
3	177	3	12	358	4
4	384	4	13	181	3
5	466	4	14	467	4
6	393	4	15	449	4
7	442	4	16	507	5
8	219	3	17	137	3
9	583	5	18	447	4
Out	3,588	36	In	3,505	36
			Total	7,093	72

You don't have to hold your breath for the course to kick in on the 17th. One of the best holes is the reachable par-5 2nd. With palm trees lining the fairway an accurate draw is required from the tee. The hole is deliberately kept at a realistic length so that it is hittable in two, but the second shot is played to one of Dye's trademark small greens, with penalizing rough and pot bunkers offering ample protection.

Recent alterations to the course have emphasized the 'hard and fast' style of the design. The result of this is that a wayward shot now has even more chance of running away into trouble, which has been increased through the addition of 200 newly planted trees. The length of the course has changed little since it was first built, only about 200 yards/183 m having been added in nearly 30 years. The emphasis, then, is on creating exciting golf through reachable distances – refreshing in an era when too many other courses are put on steroids for tour events! The biggest change is a new clubhouse in the 'stately home' style.

ABOVE AND RIGHT *The 17th hole has acquired a notoriety all of its own. On the opening day of the Players Championship in 1984 no fewer than 64 balls were hit into the water under blustery conditions. The stroke average was 3.79, making it the hardest par 3 in Tour history to that date.*

Banff Springs

Stanley Thompson 18, Fairmont Banff Springs Hotel, Banff, Alberta, Canada

Early golf courses simply evolved. Golfers found a route through whatever natural obstacles they found where they had chosen to play. There was minimal earth moving. The emergence of the earliest course architects, such as Old Tom Morris, towards the end of the 19th century was accompanied by earth moving on a very small scale – as much as a couple of men with shovels or possibly with a horse and scraper could move. Enter the steam shovel. It could hardly move mountains, but it could shift a large amount of dirt in a day. Throw in dynamite and almost anything became possible, or it did if you had a huge budget.

The enormous Banff Springs Hotel belonged to the Canadian Pacific Railway (CPR). It was the jewel in their crown, standing proudly overlooking the Spray and Bow Rivers surrounded by the stunning scenery of the Rocky Mountains. It had had a golf course of sorts since 1911 but it hardly matched up to the rest of the facilities on offer at this world-class hotel. The CPR had money and they also had railway trucks, trainloads of them. They had seen what Canadian architect Stanley Thompson had achieved at their rival railway Canadian National's resort at Jasper Park, so they hired Thompson themselves.

LUCKY ACCIDENT

Banff's most famous hole, the 4th, Devil's Cauldron, was not part of Thompson's original plan. He had no intention of using this area of the extensive property. However, during the winter of 1927, when heavy snows and bitter temperatures had halted construction work, an avalanche created a new glacial lake. When Thompson returned to Banff he spotted the lake and its potential as the basis for a world-class short hole immediately.

LEFT AND BELOW
*Wonderful golf in an exquisite
setting. Stanley Thompson's
course at Banff Springs is
exceptional – the 4th hole is,
quite simply, one of the
greatest holes in golf.*

The world's most expensive golf course

It took Thompson and his team two years to build the Banff course, and when it opened in 1929 it was said to be the most expensive course ever built. The great thing about the course is that you would never guess that Thompson had spent so much money and moved so many thousands of tons of earth, for it all looks so natural. And what the unsuspecting eye might not notice is that a lot of Thompson's creativity went into ensuring that manufactured features, such as bunkers, raised greens and mounds, were perfectly scaled to the grandeur of the surrounding forests and mountains. As a result of such empathy, the course is not overwhelmed by the scenery.

In recent years a new clubhouse has been erected and the original order of playing the holes abandoned. So the course now starts with a hole that throws the golfer straight into the forests. The next two holes turn to face Mount Rundle. Thompson needed dynamite to blast away enough room to build the 3rd fairway. Further dynamite was required to clear the site for the 4th green, but it was well worth it, for the 4th is a world-class short hole (so good that *Golf Magazine* ranks it in the top four in the world), calling for a drop-shot down over a glacial lake to find a well-bunkered green on the far side. After three more holes in the forests the course emerges for a sequence of beautiful holes alongside the Bow River.

Thompson's original opening hole is now the 15th and many an experienced golfer has stood on that tee and been knocked off their game by the sight ahead, with the sparkling Spray River far below and the tree-lined and bunker-strewn fairway uncomfortably distant on its far side.

CARD OF THE COURSE

Hole	Distance (yards)	Par
1	415	4
2	180	3
3	535	5
4	200	3
5	430	4
6	380	4
7	610	5
8	160	3
9	510	5
Out	3,420	36
10	225	3
11	425	4
12	450	4
13	230	3
14	445	4
15	480	4
16	420	4
17	385	4
18	585	5
In	3,645	35
Total	7,065	71

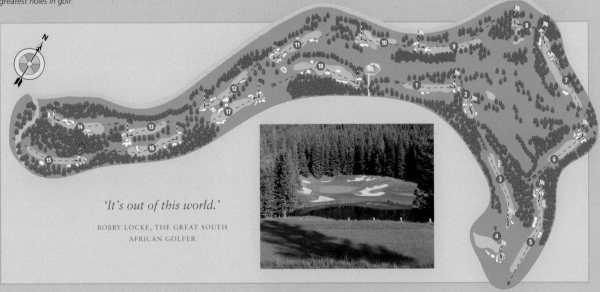

'It's out of this world.'

BOBBY LOCKE, THE GREAT SOUTH
AFRICAN GOLFER

Cabo del Sol

Ocean Course, Cabo del Sol Golf Club, Baja California, Mexico

Baja California, with its enviable climate (350 days of sun per year), was bound to catch on as a holiday resort at some point. As far as the Mexicans were concerned it might as well have been another country, for apart from a tiny strip of continuous land at the very north of the peninsula it is separated from the mainland by the many hundreds of miles of the Sea of Cortes.

The Americans and Canadians solved its accessibility problems by flying in, which they now do in considerable numbers, in the early days to fish or whale-watch. It was inevitable that they would want to play golf, too, and the two contrasting courses at Cabo del Sol provided a very potent seed from which further developments are arising.

To confirm to the travelling public that Cabo del Sol is a top-of-the-range resort, two of the great names of golf course design were commissioned to lay out courses – Jack Nicklaus and Tom Weiskopf. Nicklaus was unquestionably the greatest golfer of his era (many would say of all time) and a master player at demolishing a golf course, but his own-design courses are more generous to the average

player than you might expect. He took to heart the adverse criticisms of his early designs, 'too hard and made for Nicklaus'. Weiskopf, on the other hand, had one of the most elegant swings of all time and a formidable technique, yet did not achieve as many major results as were once forecast. His golf courses, however, are frequently far more thought-provoking than those of some of the more prolific winners among his contemporaries.

BELOW *The 17th hole, played across the beach even from the very front tees, is beautifully routed to align with the distant peaks.*

CARD OF THE COURSE

Hole	Distance (yards)	Par
1	436	4
2	574	5
3	327	4
4	555	5
5	458	4
6	190	3
7	207	3
8	438	4
9	469	4
Out	3,654	36
10	436	4
11	352	4
12	515	5
13	213	3
14	366	4
15	530	5
16	429	4
17	178	3
18	430	4
In	3,449	36
Total	7,103	72

▶ Although golf tourism is relatively new to this part of Mexico, tourists of another kind colonized the area in the 1730s: the Spanish, who established a presidio in San José del Cabo. Nor are modern tourists only golfers – fishing is big here, too.

ABOVE RIGHT *The 13th, the only inland par 3 on the Ocean Course, is a fine hole, played downhill to a green defended by bunkers, cacti and scrub.*

Desert and ocean

Cabo boasts two completely different styles of course. Weiskopf's Desert Course was built inland, a rugged course (admittedly with fine ocean views) that asks the golfer contemporary questions of length, accuracy and finesse. Nicklaus's Ocean Course is in many ways gentler, although there are compulsory carries over the Pacific on the 5th and 7th, 17th and 18th holes. Yet, to the competent player, water carries are hardly intimidating. What the good player might enjoy more is the challenge of the approach shots to the 5th and 16th, whose greens are deceptively set up on the very edge of the ocean and therefore call into question the golfer's trust in the yardage and commitment to the shot. Psychological golf can be such fun!

The Jockey Club

The Jockey Club, San Isidro, Buenos Aires, Argentina

At the 2007 US Open, the world found out that Argentinian golf is seriously underrated as Angel Cabrera stormed to victory; the same goes for Argentinian golf courses. Few would consider this country for a golfing break, but the region is home to some fine courses, the best being the Jockey Club.

Founded in 1882 for the polo-playing social elite, the club decided to add golf to its activities in the 1920s. Wisely, they hired Alister MacKenzie (who already had Royal Melbourne and Cypress Point in his portfolio) to design two courses on an area of land they had purchased. MacKenzie accepted, pleased to escape from the depression engulfing the United States where he was then living, but he soon found himself staring at a grimly flat landscape. His solution was to create the signature features of both courses: the countless artificial mounds that adorn both fairways and greens. MacKenzie adored St Andrews and he recaptured much of its spirit on this very dissimilar terrain. It is often said that golf course architects should be judged by their work on unpromising land. MacKenzie robustly proves that contention here.

The Blue Course is the shorter of the two, and accuracy is called for to navigate its tight fairways. In a final salute to St Andrews, the 9th and 18th greens are joined together to create a stunning double green, divided by one of the many substantial mounds. Though both courses are similar, it is the longer Red Course that has seen tournament action, including the 2001 Argentine Open, won by none other than Angel Cabrera.

RIGHT *The extraordinary mounds surrounding the 16th green are closely shaven to give multiple options for a recovery shot.*

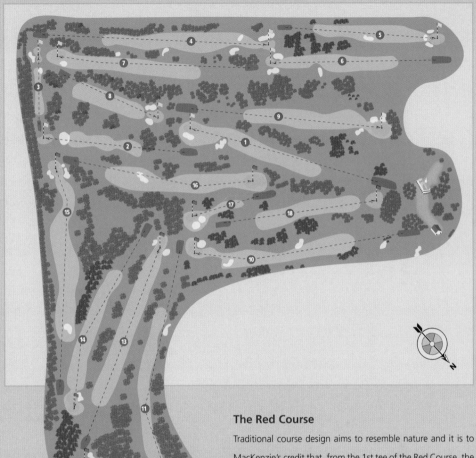

In 2005 Kevin Stadler won the Argentine Open (in its centenary year) at the Jockey Club to become the only father/son winners in the tournament's history – his father, Craig, having triumphed in 1992.

CARD OF THE COURSE

Hole	Distance (yards)	Par	Hole	Distance (yards)	Par
1	425	4	10	470	4
2	350	4	11	506	5
3	148	3	12	175	3
4	490	5	13	444	4
5	340	4	14	390	4
6	355	4	15	511	5
7	425	4	16	401	4
8	208	3	17	170	3
9	415	4	18	354	4
Out	3,156	35	In	3,421	36
			Total	6,577	71

The Red Course

Traditional course design aims to resemble nature and it is to MacKenzie's credit that, from the 1st tee of the Red Course, the mounds sweeping the fairway look entirely natural. It is also apparent that these mounds are a major strategic feature, many easily as tall as a golfer, and there will rarely be a flat lie or straight fairway roll. That is not to say that the course is needlessly penalizing. MacKenzie designed courses to be enjoyable to play, and this becomes evident on the 2nd. At just 350 yards/320 m, this is far from the slog of too much modern design, but the hole must be played with skill as the green is mountainous. Creativity is called for, with the design urging players to dream up running shots and long-range putts in true links spirit. The undulations provide such a thorough test that it was even debated whether the course needed bunkers at all.

Today the Jockey Club represents something of an oasis. When you walk down the bunkerless 18th, backed by the thumping of thoroughbred hooves from the adjacent polo field and racecourse, it is hard not to be smitten with the traditional atmosphere. This charming course has something different to offer to the more distance-orientated modern game. Argentina truly is an underrated golfing destination.

Le Golf National

Le Golf National

L'Albatros Course, Le Golf National, Guyancourt, France

Built on flat land, nowhere near the sea, and with 353,000 cubic yards/270,000 cubic metres of artificial lakes, it may seem preposterous to liken Le Golf National to a Scottish links. But when the wind gusts over the dunes, through the ashen rough and straight into your face, the similarities become clear. In true links fashion, the course is open to the elements, but the design also features the lakes and stadium golf of an American TPC course. It is this mix of styles that creates the course's main defence, as one is called upon to be creative, playing links shots as well as target golf.

Popular French golf only really took off in the 1970s when the economic potential of the game was realized. Courses sprang up all over the place, spearheaded by a new wave of course architects. The effects of this golfing revolution are apparent today, with a sudden influx of good French professionals. Le Golf National is probably the most important course to come out of this era, becoming the permanent home to the French Open Championship.

The course must have seemed somewhat of a gamble when it was proposed. Not only was the country new to the golfing buzz, but the land was also far too flat to fulfil the brief: to create France's first course capable of hosting regular tournaments. Two years later, after the transportation of 400 trucks of earth a day, the course was both undulating and teeming with bunkers and lakes, and plentiful spectator mounds.

RIGHT *In many respects this bleak, windswept site resembles a links, but what it cannot have is true links turf and genuine seaside sand dunes.*

▶ There is a shorter 18-hole course, L'Aigle, which has a distinctly Scottish feel to it, and a charming nine-hole course for training.

BELOW *The short 16th is one of several holes on the back nine with treacherous water carries.*

'All the shots you have to play

offer multiple choices.'

SEVE BALLESTEROS

CARD OF THE COURSE

Hole	Distance (yards)	Par	Hole	Distance (yards)	Par
1	415	4	10	377	4
2	202	3	11	191	3
3	530	5	12	437	4
4	439	4	13	410	4
5	404	4	14	552	5
6	377	4	15	421	4
7	443	4	16	175	3
8	207	3	17	470	4
9	563	5	18	514	5
Out	3,580	36	In	3,547	36
			Total	7,127	72

Scotland meets Florida

All these features are apparent from the 1st tee.

The fairway is narrowed by a large lake on the left, which also adds intimidation to the approach shot. Bunkers mark the right-hand edge of the fairway before the land turns to dunes. At 415 yards/379 m, position is more important than length, and a 3-wood down the right-hand side gives the best line at the enormously long green. From here there is great diversity in holes, but one must take early birdie chances, as the course gets consistently harder.

Looking down the fairway from the 15th tee, you really could be in Florida, with an expansive lake on the right dwarfing the playing surface. Inevitably most shots are played too cautiously down the left, but this leaves a long approach to a green almost surrounded by the vast lake. In the 1991 French Open, seven balls were lost in the lake by a three-ball!

On the opposite side of the lake, the 18th is almost a mirror image of the 15th. Water stretches all the way down the left side of this par 5. But the fairway is wide and, with a relatively easy approach over the water, it is possible to finish in style. Unlike Retief Goosen, who was five shots clear on the tee in 1997 and opted to lay up short of the water. He topped the ball into the water and finished with a seven to win by only three!

Sporting Club Berlin

Faldo Course, Sporting Club Berlin, Bad Sarrow, Germany

Before World War II, Germany could boast more golf courses than any other country in continental Europe. After the war the country was divided and the eastern part, the DDR, became aligned with Soviet Russia. Golf and Communism were not compatible and a number of fine old courses were abandoned, never to be restored. As an island city, surrounded by Communist territory, Berlin could not expand. It boasted a single 18-hole course and there was no possibility of room being found for any other course within the western-controlled sectors.

The fall of Communism and the symbolic dismantling of the Berlin Wall provided a stimulus for the rapid development of new courses within easy striking range of the city on former DDR territory. Given that agricultural practices in the DDR were antiquated and that much farm work was still carried out using horses it seems a pity that no developer thought to exploit those skills while they remained available in order to create a traditional course such as Colt or Simpson might have built. The results are so much subtler. Instead, developers have seen this as an opportunity to aim for the high-end market, and top of that list is the impressive resort at Bad Sarrow, Sporting Club Berlin.

RIGHT *A view of the par-5 10th hole on the Faldo Course at Bad Saarow. Faldo has a great affinity with links golf. It shows here.*

▶ The back nine of the Palmer-designed Champions Course runs into the woods and has been described as the most beautiful back nine in Germany.

ABOVE *Escape from the bunkers on the Faldo Course needs strength, skill, commitment and nerve. These are on the 17th.*

Big name designers

You can add millions of dollars to the construction bill for a new course if you persuade a famous golfer to put his name to the design. For that money you might get two or three single-day visits from the great man, the design work being carried out by the full-time architects in his team. Nick Faldo is something of an exception, taking a rather greater personal interest in the detailed design of 'his' courses than most. His links-like course at Bad Sarrow has already attracted much favourable comment. It makes a fine contrast with the Arnold Palmer woodland course at the same resort. There is a third 18-hole course by Stan Eby, plus exemplary practice facilities.

The Faldo Course was intended to hold professional tournaments right from the start (it has hosted a number of German Opens), but Faldo was not to be tempted to make this course a long slog. Interestingly, he has included a number of shorter par 4s in the repertoire, and water – the seemingly obligatory element of any new design with championship aspirations – is blissfully absent, being a factor only on the par-5 1st and 10th holes. It could hardly be a links course without bunkers and Faldo has seen to it that there are 133 of them, most of the deep pot-bunker variety.

Flat the land may be, but there are abundant features to the course, with angled greens such as at the 7th, narrow entrances to them such as at the 9th, and always the thought that if you finish in the wrong part of one of these bunkers you are almost bound to lose a stroke.

▶ SC Berlin is not just about golf. It is one of Europe's finest sports resorts, offering tennis, riding, sailing on the largest lake in Brandenburg and excellent spa facilities.

CARD OF THE COURSE

Hole	Distance (yards)	Par	Hole	Distance (yards)	Par
1	548	5	10	559	5
2	414	4	11	570	5
3	186	3	12	376	4
4	379	4	13	233	3
5	213	3	14	415	4
6	533	5	15	391	4
7	439	4	16	360	4
8	382	4	17	193	3
9	447	4	18	458	4
Out	3,541	36	In	3,555	36
			Total	7,096	72

San Lorenzo

San Lorenzo Golf Course, Almancil, Algarve, Portugal

The Algarve is one of the most popular golfing destinations in Europe. It has the climate to be wonderfully attractive to Northern European golfers during the dark and cold winter months, yet Atlantic breezes help to prevent it from being unbearably hot during the summer. Golf courses litter the region – the choice is immense. But there is another side to it. The Algarve is now a maze of concrete, high-rise apartment blocks. To enjoy golf in the Algarve it is necessary to be very selective, and the course that has that little bit of edge over the others is San Lorenzo.

San Lorenzo dates from the late 1980s, a design by the American architect Joe Lee. What Lee had in his favour was a site that descends to the Atlantic Ocean and he made full use of the advantage he was given. There is another plus, it must be said. Like all other Algarve courses, San Lorenzo is woven between real-estate developments. The developments here, however, are of Hollywood-style villas and mansions adorned with Moorish ornaments. They may resemble a film set, but they are far superior to the dreaded high-rise monstrosities elsewhere.

Nature's backdrop

It is not quite true to say that San Lorenzo descends to the Atlantic Ocean. More correctly, it descends to the banks of the estuary of the Ria Formosa, which is separated from the ocean by a low ridge of sand dunes. The shelter these dunes afford to the estuary ensures a safe haven for a wide range of species of swimming, diving and wading birds. Happily, the whole area is designated a nature reserve.

While ornithologists may rush to the 6th and 7th holes, so do golfers, for it is at this point that San Lorenzo comes into its own. Both holes enjoy elevated teeing grounds from which drives are made on to narrow strips of fairway bordering the waters. There are no marks for playing too safe – the chances of finding the ball on the tree-clad hills on the left are no better than 50:50. Both greens lie perilously close to the beach, that on the 7th, unusually, bunkered behind.

For the average golfer, the 8th is about keeping out of trouble and using any handicap shots available – it is, after all, Stroke 3. But for the big hitter it is an exciting hole, with water all the way down the right and hillocks encroaching from the left where you would rather they did not.

The back nine opens with a demanding drive over an arm of a lagoon to a rising, curving fairway, but from here on – until the 17th – the round is solid rather than spectacular, handicap golfers inventing their own problems. At the 17th, however, the prospect of a watery grave looms, or else dropping a shot by playing too safely away from the lagoon. The green is threatened by water. So is the 18th green, but this time there is no safe route for the timid. At some point at least one stretch of water must be taken on and conquered.

LEFT *San Lorenzo's final green, surrounded by water and sand, is a difficult target whatever the length of the approach shot – a touch of Florida in the Algarve.*

CARD OF THE COURSE

Hole	Distance (yards)	Par
1	540	5
2	177	3
3	365	4
4	372	4
5	143	3
6	422	4
7	377	4
8	574	5
9	400	4
Out	3,370	36
10	568	5
11	383	4
12	432	4
13	393	4
14	172	3
15	517	5
16	208	3
17	376	4
18	406	4
In	3,455	36
Total	**6,825**	**72**

▶ San Lorenzo has never sought to attract professional tournament golf, and has been spared the unnatural lengthening so often imposed on Tour courses.

▶ San Lorenzo is located within the Quinta do Lago estate, although it is not part of the Quinta do Lago portfolio that includes the four Quinta courses and two Vale de Lobo courses.

PORTUGUESE RESORT GOLF

Portugal's rise in prominence from being an almost golfless country to that of being a major player in resort golf is quite remarkable. Suffice it to say that there were only three courses on mainland Portugal at the end of World War II. There are now over 50 courses and the number is rising steadily, even alarmingly. Yet this is almost entirely a business for tourists, and given the winter climate of northern Europe one understands why it should be so. In comparison with the number of golf courses there are few native players. The sad thing about this is that golf courses are developed in an 'international' style for 'international' golfers.

A comparison can be made with Vinho Verde, a Portuguese wine of no greatness, but the perfect accompaniment to *bacalhau*, that great Portuguese salt-cod dish. Have the real thing served to you in a jug and it is frothing, bone dry and utterly thirst-quenching. Drink the stuff made for tourists and it is semi-sweet, a little cloying and bottled with a fancy label. It loses its character and its honesty. Portuguese resort courses need a little more distinctive character and rather fewer fancy labels.

RIGHT *The 6th green is found only after a perfect drive from an elevated tee to a low fairway bounded by a treacherous, scrub-clad hill and the Ria Formosa.*

ABOVE RIGHT *Unusual bunkering is a feature of the 7th green, its purpose, as much as anything, to deceive the eye into thinking the target is smaller.*

Valderrama

Club de Golfe Valderrama, San Roque, Cadiz, Spain

Regarded by many as the top golf course in continental Europe, Valderrama is inextricably linked with the Volvo Masters, the European Tour's end-of-season flagship event. In 1997 it hosted one of the most closely fought Ryder Cups, with Seve Ballesteros's European team managing to withstand the comeback of the Americans on the final day to retain the Cup by a margin of one point. Despite its high profile, and the menacing reputation of the 17th, Valderrama prides itself on being playable by all skill levels. A large range of tees ensures not only widely differing yardages, but also different routings, to cater to various abilities. Credit must go to the inventive design of the course, which, interestingly, was designed twice by the same man.

Valderrama began its life as the New Course at Sotogrande, in turn becoming Las Aves, before being bought by rich Bolivian industrialist, Jaime Ortiz-Patiño. Keen to host high-quality tournament golf, Ortiz-Patiño called back the designer of the course – the prolific architect Robert Trent Jones – to make alterations. Most significant of these changes was to reverse the two nines so the hardest run of holes would become the finishing stretch. A massive drainage programme was initiated and, later, a lake was introduced in front of the 17th green. Conditioning is always impeccable.

Shades of Augusta

Overall length has never been a priority at Valderrama but the challenges are considerable. The course is hilly, wind is a constant factor – and a variable one, with two prevailing winds changing the characteristics of the course from day to day – and a proliferation of trees makes particularly high demands on straight hitting. The trees remove options from play. Usually there is only one specific route to the green, meaning that this is target golf.

One of Ortiz-Patiño's aims was to replicate the feel of Augusta, both in condition and design, and this is achieved well on the 10th. Despite its short length, there is little room for error as the tee shot must be faded past a lake on the right and short of a bunker that devours a tee shot hit too straight. From here one has a magnificent view of the green, surrounded by white sand bunkers and a ring of cork trees. But, like the 9th at Augusta, the approach must be hit positively, as a weak shot will roll backwards off the green and often back down the fairway!

The environment plays an important role in the Valderrama experience, and the natural beauty of the course is a shining example to others. An active involvement in ecology means that there are twice as many species of plant and a third as many more types of bird on the course than in the surrounding countryside. While many courses resort to fertilizer, pesticide and even dyeing the lakes blue, Valderrama has maintained quality without neglecting the environment. In fact, US Ryder Cup captain Tom Kite claimed the greens to be among the best he had ever putted on.

▶ Huge sums are spent each year on maintaining the course in peak condition. Valderrama has 4,600 sprinklers, compared to the 600 for the average course in the United States.

LEFT *This view of the short par-4 10th shows why yardages are irrelevant, even at professional level, if the topography of the site and the intuition of the architect are in harmony.*

CARD OF THE COURSE

Hole	Distance (yards)	Par
1	389	4
2	399	4
3	173	3
4	535	5
5	381	4
6	163	3
7	461	4
8	345	4
9	441	4
Out	3,287	35
10	364	4
11	547	5
12	197	3
13	402	4
14	370	4
15	200	3
16	422	4
17	511	5
18	434	4
In	3,447	36
Total	6,734	71

'Awesome.'

FRED COUPLES, ON HIS FIRST
GLIMPSE OF VALDERRAMA

N

Crans-sur-Sierre

Golf Club Crans-sur-Sierre, Valais, Switzerland

The European Masters and, before it, the Swiss Open have attracted quality fields to Crans-sur-Sierre every year since 1948, plus the one prewar Swiss Open held at Crans in 1939. It has produced some famous winners: Garcia, Donald, Els, Romero, Westwood, Montgomerie, Ballesteros, Olazábal, Stadler, Faldo, Woosnam, Price, Locke, Rees, Nagle and Charles to name but a few. They enjoy playing here: they like the place; they like the atmosphere; they like the winner's cheque; they like the golf course. After all, it usually produces very low scoring.

The first course at Crans was set up in 1905, opening the following year with a nine-hole layout, which was expanded a few years later to 18. It did not survive World War I. A second attempt at establishing a course, again of nine holes, was made in 1921. That was superseded by an 18-hole course that opened in 1929. It was designed by an Englishman, Harry Nicholson, and remained largely intact until 1997 when Seve Ballesteros was commissioned to rebuild the greens, add a little difficulty around the course, and create some new back tees.

LOW SCORING

It was at Crans-sur-Sierre in 1971 that the Italian golfer, Baldovino Dassù, recorded a 60, the first time anyone had achieved it on the European Tour. Against the par of the day this worked out at an astonishing 13 under par. Colin Montgomerie holds the 72-hole scoring record for Crans at 260. He closed with rounds of 61 and 63 to win by four shots.

RIGHT *The 7th is one of the easiest holes on the course, a drive-and-pitch hole of only 331 yards/303 m, but who could not be exhilarated by such a spectacle!*

Stunning scenery

If you were to set down the Crans course in the middle of flat farmland it would attract little attention. It is perfectly good but nothing remarkable in itself. What sets it apart – very much apart – is the ravishing scenery. It is not every day that you get to pitch to a skyline green backed by a towering, snowy Alpine peak. Against such massive backdrops the golf course can seem minuscule. In fact it is far from minuscule, measuring a healthy 6,937 yards/6,343 m from the white tees, with a par 5 stretching to 629 yards/575 m and the longest par 4 being 503 yards/460 m. That said, the course sits at an altitude of some 5,000 feet/1,500 m which enables longer hitting.

The course opens with a reachable par 5 before doubling back for a sturdy two-shot hole, followed by a short hole along the course boundary. In the past, the 4th was played as a par 5, but now it is a super-long par 4, and even from the visitors' tees it measures a healthy 487 yards/445 m. Length is less significant on the dogleg 5th, pine-enclosed 6th, wide-open 7th and well-bunkered 8th but then comes the extraordinary 9th, wending its way relentlessly to its green near the clubhouse.

On the back nine there is another sharply doglegged hole, the 12th, and back-to-back par 5s. You and I play the 16th as a short par 4, but for the European Masters it is shortened to a 235-yard/215-m par 3, bringing the overall par down to 71. Two straightforward par 4s then bring us home.

▶ There is a second, nine-hole, course at Crans, designed by Jack Nicklaus. It is hoped eventually to extend this course to 18 holes.

▶ Crans is possibly the best example of a place where the course map, or course statistics, tell little of the golfing experience.

CARD OF THE COURSE

Hole	Distance (yards)	Par	Hole	Distance (yards)	Par
1	540	5	10	405	4
2	439	4	11	205	3
3	191	3	12	410	4
4	503	4	13	200	3
5	339	4	14	595	5
6	324	4	15	516	5
7	331	4	16	346	4
8	175	3	17	386	4
9	629	5	18	403	4
Out	3,471	36	In	3,466	36
			Total	6,937	72

Emirates

Majlis Course, Emirates Golf Club, Dubai, United Arab Emirates

The Emirates Golf Club was dubbed 'The Desert Miracle' when, in 1988, it became the first grass course in the Middle East, and it is easy to see why. Sheikh Mohammed bin Rashid Al Maktoum, of the Dubai ruling family, donated the property and urged that the course should reflect the natural state of the land. Karl Litten's design was an instant success, creating lush Bermuda-grass fairways of a kind more usually associated with Augusta National, while protecting them with the natural desert dunes.

Not only has the course succeeded in bringing grass to the desert, there are also abundant water hazards. Desalinated water is transported to the course from a nearby factory at huge engineering expense. It is achievement enough that any golf course has been constructed in such an inhospitable environment, but the fact that the course is a fine one almost makes it deserving of the accolade of a 'miracle'!

Instant recognition

The quality of the course was instantly appreciated when the European Tour chose the Majlis for the Dubai Desert Classic just one year after its completion. As a result the course can already boast a considerable history for one so relatively young. Drama is often created around the excellent 18th, a long par 5, which doglegs around a lake. A simple lay-up is sensible, but the temptation is to cut the corner and risk finding water. Then the approach shot is also over a stretch of water that has claimed the errant shots of many a great player. Both Ian Woosnam and Tiger Woods have lost the championship from near-certain victory by finding water with approaches at 18. But it is a rewarding hole if played well, perfectly demonstrated by Ernie Els, who struck a majestic 6-iron to 22 feet/7 m and rolled the putt in for eagle to claim victory by one shot in 2005.

▶ Ernie Els holds the course record 61, which helped him to victory in the 1994 Dubai Desert Classic. He also won the tournament in 2002 and 2005.

▶ Tiger Woods won the 2008 Dubai Desert Classic in stunning fashion, taking just 31 strokes on the back nine to catch and overtake Els in the final round.

LEFT *Linking the lush fairways and greens of the Majlis Course with what was once barren desert beyond, the remarkable clubhouse is styled after Bedouin tents.*

CARD OF THE COURSE

Hole	Distance (yards)	Par	Hole	Distance (yards)	Par
1	458	4	10	549	5
2	351	4	11	169	3
3	530	5	12	467	4
4	188	3	13	550	5
5	436	4	14	434	4
6	485	4	15	180	3
7	184	3	16	425	4
8	434	4	17	359	4
9	463	4	18	547	5
Out	3,529	35	In	3,680	37
			Total	7,209	72

Like the 18th, many holes require a strong nerve and a great deal of accuracy to play over the picturesque oasis-like lakes, but the best-looking hole on the course is the stunning 8th. The fairway doglegs around the desert on this difficult par 4, creating a captivating view from the tee, as lush green fairway is contrasted with desert scrub. Equally impressive is the approach shot, played to a raised green backed by the dramatic clubhouse.

The clubhouse is an extraordinary sight, built in white concrete and glass; it resembles a Bedouin tented village, providing a unique backdrop for a beautiful course. Hospitality is a matter of pride at the club, and this extends beyond the superbly equipped clubhouse. Golfers are looked after out on the course as well, even provided with air-conditioned refreshment huts – it is in the desert, after all, and temperatures range from 86–122°F/30–50°C!

In 2006 the second 18-hole course, the Wadi, was redesigned by Nick Faldo. This course is also appealing, incorporating the 'wadi' (Arabic for 'valley') into the design, which, along with Faldo's trademark fairway bunkering, creates an interesting course requiring disciplined course management.

Fancourt

The Links at Fancourt, Fancourt Hotel and Country Club Estate, George, South Africa

Late on 23 November 2003, the Links played host to one of golf's greatest duels. The US and International teams of the President's Cup, tied at the end of four days of golf, sent one player each to settle the match with a head-to-head, sudden death play-off. An estimated 800 million people worldwide watched Ernie Els and Tiger Woods battle for the cup as darkness fell on the picturesque course.

With the first two holes halved, both players faced long par-saving putts on the third play-off hole. Tiger holed out from 15 feet/4.5 m to leave Els with a putt of 8 feet/2.5 m to keep the match alive. Opposing captain Jack Nicklaus later said, 'There wasn't anybody in the world who wanted to see you miss that putt,' and Els duly rose above the pressure and holed out. Captains Nicklaus and Player epitomized the spirit of the game by agreeing to a tie and sharing the cup.

Designed by Gary Player, this strikingly beautiful course sweeps through mounds at the feet of the Outeniqua Mountains, the dunes creating a links-like experience.

These mounds are often assumed to be natural because they seem so in keeping with the surrounding mountains, but they are actually the result of a huge amount of earth moving. In fact, from the mounds down the right of the 13th, there is a good view of the flat farmland that is the land's more natural state. But natural or not, the course plays like a links, those carefully created mounds enveloping the fairways and fierce pot bunkers protecting tough greens.

BELOW *The clubhouse at Fancourt reflects the atmosphere of the Manor House, the hub of the resort, where fine dining is the order of the day.*

Risk and reward

Player's trademark design features – risk and reward and playability to all skill levels – exist throughout the course. Powerful hitters have opportunities to make long carries on most holes, and there is temptation to drive both short par 4s, the 6th and 14th. However, the drives must be perfect as the holes are cleverly designed, with large pot bunkers and thick rough on the dunes ready to gobble up wild shots.

Multiple tees successfully keep the course interesting to all golfers, so an exciting contest will arise between a long hitter and a short accurate player. On all too many other courses the holes are consistently too tight for the long hitter, or too long for the player relying on accuracy. It is this element of the design that made the course perfect for the matchplay of the President's Cup, as one player could lay up safely in the fairway, allowing his partner to take on the aggressive lines.

The long par-4 15th is reminiscent of the 18th at Sawgrass, doglegging left around marshland. However, the unsung hero is the par-3 17th. With a stone-walled burn short and left, most golfers play out to the right, leaving themselves a tough chip across a slick green. Trees behind the green add confusion about wind direction. This is when you should turn for advice to one of the caddies at Fancourt, said to be among the best in the world.

FANCOURT'S FOUR COURSES

The Links is the highest profile of four courses at Fancourt. The Montagu has recently been upgraded by David McClay Kidd, designer of Bandon Dunes in Oregon, USA, while the Outeniqua is a 7,000-yard/6,400-m Gary Player design. To play these courses you must stay at the resort. The public-access course is Bramble Hill, designed by Player to give 'golfers of every level a Fancourt experience'.

CARD OF THE COURSE

Hole	Distance (yards)	Par
1	396	4
2	236	3
3	469	4
4	494	4
5	549	5
6	341	4
7	476	4
8	202	3
9	609	5
Out	3,772	36
10	408	4
11	161	3
12	481	4
13	533	5
14	361	4
15	477	4
16	584	5
17	186	3
18	616	5
In	3,807	37
Total	7,579	73

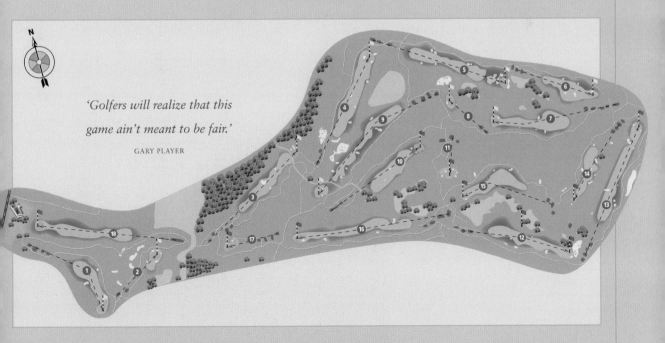

'Golfers will realize that this game ain't meant to be fair.'
GARY PLAYER

Fancourt

In order to get the links feel just right,
Player (rumoured to be the world's most
travelled athlete) revisited a number of
links courses in Scotland and Ireland.
Writing about Fancourt, he said, 'It has
been designed to make golfers feel as
though they were at Ballybunion, Dornoch
or St Andrews, with rolling fairways, pot
bunkers, big greens, high rough and a
seascape appearance.'

ABOVE *The 17th, viewed
here from left of the tee, is
reckoned to be one of the
toughest par 3s on all four
courses. The humps and
bumps designed to give
the course an authentic
links appearance are clearly
visible in the background.*

RIGHT *Key to producing
a links-like playing
experience is scaling the
artificial undulations so
that they are not
overwhelmed by the
mountain background,
aptly demonstrated here
on the 12th hole.*

Royal Calcutta

Royal Calcutta Golf Club, Kolkata, India

The Royal Calcutta Golf Club is the oldest in the world outside Great Britain, founded as the Dum Dum Golf Club in 1829. It was some 12 years before another Indian golf club was established, this time in Mumbai, and between them the two clubs fostered the game in the subcontinent. Indeed, Royal Calcutta (it became Royal at the time of the visit of King George V and Queen Mary to India in 1911) was so influential that it had a status similar to the R&A in that it was the custodian of the rules and etiquette of the game in India. The club also set up the Amateur Championship for India.

Under British rule, Royal Calcutta excluded Indian members. Happily that is no longer the case, although the club still retains its strong links with the R&A and also with a number of British clubs with which it shares reciprocal courtesy of the course. Less happily, however, the club could not afford to retain all of its former 36-hole grounds, selling off that portion further from the clubhouse to the Bengal government. What remains, however, is a formidable 18-hole test.

Unseen dangers

At first sight, Royal Calcutta appears to be benign, with flat fairways and few bunkers. What the eye has not seen is a whole network of ponds and pools and interconnecting ditches criss-crossing the course below the level of the fairway. They were created when earth was dug out to form the greens and tees and, as they are now used to store water, are known as tanks. Their positions cannot be predicted and there may be several forced carries over them on any hole.

One of the hardest holes on the course is the 7th, a solid par 4 running along the course boundary, driving out of a chute of trees towards a fairway curving to the left past water, before another tank cuts the fairway off abruptly. With the length of the drive limited, the second shot is substantial. Another strong hole on the way out is the 3rd, curving this time to the right, with a serious carry over a tank to find the fairway.

Royal Calcutta is a long course, but this is largely because, like the Old Course at St Andrews, there are only two short

RIGHT *The splendid clubhouse, which has been the spiritual home of Indian golf since 1829. It still carries with it a sense of grandeur and formality.*

holes. The par 5s are not particularly long by today's standards, but there are enough longer par 4s to keep mid- and long-irons in work. A good example is the 10th, which, yet again, involves a second shot that must carry water in front of the pear-shaped green. And so it goes on, tank after tank, until suddenly, on the last hole, there is water-free fairway. Surely there must be one more hidden tank lurking to catch the incautious somewhere before the green! But no, a single fairway bunker and a couple of greenside ones are all that remain to trap the unwary.

▶ The Cashmere Cup, presented by Royal Calcutta Golf Club to the R&A in 1882, became the trophy for the world's first handicap tournament, now known as the Calcutta Cup.

RIGHT *Sheep sheltering from the heat of the sun in a bunker at Royal Calcutta. Sheep sheltering from the wind in Scotland created many of the very first bunkers.*

CARD OF THE COURSE

Hole	Distance (yards)	Par
1	359	4
2	141	3
3	436	4
4	525	5
5	426	4
6	422	4
7	415	4
8	413	4
9	398	4
Out	3,535	36
10	432	4
11	410	4
12	369	4
13	194	3
14	409	4
15	502	5
16	362	4
17	371	4
18	430	4
In	3,479	36
Total	7,014	72

Mission Hills

Olazábal Course, Mission Hills Golf Club, Shenzhen, China

With 216 holes of golf stretched over 12 courses, each one carrying the name of a great golfer, Mission Hills is already established as the largest golf resort in the world. The names – or most of them – trip off the tongue: Annika, Duval, Els, Faldo, Leadbetter, Nicklaus, Norman, Olazábal, Ozaki, Pete Dye, Vijay and Zhang Lian Wei. The Nicklaus Course hosted the World Cup of 1995, the first time a Chinese course had been accredited by the US PGA. The tournament returned in 2007, but this time it was to be the first of 12 World Cups to be staged annually at the resort.

It is astonishing to see the way in which China has embraced golf. Whether charging in, building courses and resorts at an alarming rate, will be good for Chinese golf is yet to be seen, but its enormous tourism potential must be obvious to all. Mission Hills has the desirable asset of being a mere 20 minutes from Hong Kong, and the transport links necessary to get the numbers of visitors required to make a resort on this scale viable are excellent. Another great asset is the climate, which is good for golf all year round, as players in Hong Kong have known since golf arrived in 1889.

Long and heavily bunkered

For the 2007 World Cup the Olazábal Course was selected as the host. Olazábal has never been the longest (or most accurate) driver on tour, although he is an exceptionally gifted iron player. So it is something of a surprise to find that the course that bears his name is the longest of all 12 courses at Mission Hills. On this occasion it produced Scottish winners (for the first time since the tournament began as the Canada Cup in 1953) in Colin Montgomerie and Marc Warren, who had finished second in the previous year.

The long 6th, with its narrow fairway in the driving area, is probably the toughest of the par 4s. Like so many holes here the jungle background is impressive. There is a chance to enjoy this from the elevated tees of the 8th, a long and difficult par 3, and the 9th, a very heavily bunkered par 5. Olazábal is an impressive bunker player and this is reflected in the number of bunkers on the course – around 150. A large number of them appear on the 10th, the great majority of those littering the left side of the short but uphill par 4.

These days it is almost obligatory to provide a so-called signature hole. On the Olazábal Course this is the 15th. It is an all-out skirmish with the water that runs down the left of the fairway, giving the brave (or stupid) several options for cutting the corner to turn a regular par 5 into a death-defying two-shotter. This style of hole is becoming commonplace, as are imitations of the final hole at TPC Sawgrass, and there is a striking resemblance to this template with the last hole on the Olazábal Course, water again threatening throughout on the left.

▶ When Olazábal visited his course during construction in 2002 he was told that his and four other courses had to be finished within one year. They were – some 3,000 workers and 600 machines were brought in to do the work.

ABOVE LEFT *The 16th green on the Faldo Course bears a striking resemblance to the 17th at TPC at Sawgrass.*

BELOW LEFT *Sand is an ever-present threat on the Olazábal Course's signature hole, the 15th.*

CARD OF THE COURSE

Hole	Distance (yards)	Par
1	447	4
2	175	3
3	548	5
4	405	4
5	176	3
6	476	4
7	566	5
8	214	3
9	573	5
Out	3,580	36
10	404	4
11	568	5
12	457	4
13	241	3
14	401	4
15	580	5
16	432	4
17	197	3
18	460	4
In	3,740	36
Total	7,320	72

'This is truly a wonderful course.'

COLIN MONTGOMERIE

Blue Canyon

Blue Canyon

Canyon Course, Blue Canyon Country Club, Phuket, Thailand

Thailand is awash with golf courses, some good, some very good. The most celebrated of them all is Blue Canyon, a country club with two brilliant courses, situated in a heavenly spot looking out on to the blue waters of the Andaman Sea, with the Phang Nga mountains creating an inviting terrestrial backdrop. It is fabulously beautiful, but it was not always so. In former times this was a tin mine and rubber plantation.

When it was decided to develop a golf course here, Yoshikazu Kato was engaged as course architect, with a brief to keep the shifting of earth to a minimum and to utilize the natural features of the property. He had been given a helping hand with honouring his brief because huge quantities of earth had already been moved in the tin-mining days and the abandoned workings had filled with the rainwater that falls so abundantly in Thailand to form a network of lakes and ponds. In this climate the rapidly growing vegetation also assists in softening the once stark features. Kato began with the Canyon Course, which was built in 1991. The Lakes Course followed in 1999 and more than lives up to its name – there are water hazards on 17 of the 18 holes.

TIGER TRIUMPHANT

The 1994 Johnnie Walker Classic was played on the Canyon Course. Greg Norman stormed round the course on the final day in 64 for victory. Finishing in a tie for 34th place was a young amateur, Tiger Woods. Woods, now a professional, returned to Blue Canyon for the 1998 Johnnie Walker Classic. He began the last round nine shots behind the leader, Ernie Els, dug deep and caught up with Els on the final green. Woods won the play-off. It was an immensely popular victory, not least because Tiger's mother is herself from Thailand.

The Canyon Course

After a reasonably straightforward opening hole, water is encountered for the first time on the 2nd hole, a par 3 of some length. On the 3rd a huge calabash tree, standing in the middle of the fairway, confronts the golfer. Which way round it do you go? Accuracy off the tee and precise approach shots to tiered greens are called for on the otherwise fairly short par 4s going to the turn, while the stiff par 5s are a foretaste of the challenges ahead.

The sea views from the 10th tee are superb while the hole itself is a manageable dogleg to the left. Then comes a 600-yard/549-m monster of a par 5, with water adding complications for the long hitter. Water is present on the next hole as well, and there are strategic decisions concerning water to be made on the par-3 14th, with its kidney-shaped island green, and the 15th, too. The 17th, squeezed between trees to the left and water to the right, is an outstanding short hole, while the water-troubled 18th ensures that the pressure is kept up right to the very end of this delightful course.

LEFT *The 14th is a deceptive hole, playing shorter than you think because of the big drop from tee to green, and it can be complicated by crosswinds.*

BELOW *The strong finishing hole, with its drive over water and cunningly sloped green.*

'One of the best I have ever played on.'

TIGER WOODS, JOHNNIE WALKER CLASSIC, 1998

CARD OF THE COURSE

Hole	Distance (yards)	Par
1	390	4
2	218	3
3	449	4
4	407	4
5	398	4
6	556	5
7	205	3
8	412	4
9	561	5
Out	3,596	36
10	392	4
11	600	5
12	440	4
13	390	4
14	194	3
15	586	5
16	357	4
17	221	3
18	403	4
In	3,583	36
Total	7,179	72

Royal Melbourne

West Course, Royal Melbourne Golf Club, Black Rock, Victoria, Australia

The Royal Melbourne Golf Club has been – and still is – the most influential golf club in Australian golf. The man who made it so was a visitor, none other than Dr Alister MacKenzie. He had been sent by the R&A following a request from Royal Melbourne seeking advice on the laying out of a new course. MacKenzie arrived in October 1926, staying for two months, during which time he also visited a number of other courses, making suggestions for improvements to these courses, too.

MacKenzie's lasting influence was his recruitment of 1924 Australian Amateur champion and Royal Melbourne member, Alex Russell, and the club's greenkeeper, 'Mick' Morcom. MacKenzie was not going to be in Australia long enough to oversee the changes he suggested for so many clubs, nor would he be around to supervise at Royal Melbourne. Russell and Morcom quickly assimilated MacKenzie's architectural principles and were able to carry out a revolution in strategic design – and bunker design in particular – that has lasted to this day, especially in the Melbourne sand belt.

Model bunkers

Some years ago, when Nick Faldo, then just starting out in the golf design business, was in Australia to play in a number of tournaments, he was not to be found on the practice range in his down time. He was seen, instead, standing in, walking around, photographing and measuring many of the bunkers at Royal Melbourne, so impressed was he by their enormous variety and the huge influence they still exert on playing strategy, even though modern professionals are so expert at bunker play.

RIGHT *Both courses intertwine engagingly at Royal Melbourne. Viewed from the back of the 2nd green on the East Course, the famous 6th on the West can be seen stretching into the distance on the right.*

The bunkers are only part of the story, for the real genius of the West Course is the way MacKenzie routed the course to take maximum advantage of the topography of the site. Take, for instance, the sequence of holes from the 3rd to the 10th, which makes brilliant use of two big sandhills and two smaller ones. The 4th is a magnificent hole, whether played as a short par 5 or ultra-long par 4, with a drive over cavernous bunkers to a distant hilltop, followed by a long second shot, very likely played from a hanging lie, along a curving fairway to a heavily bunkered, distant green. Then comes the 5th, as gorgeous a short hole as you could wish to find, and the 6th is one of the world's great two-shot holes, with a drive over serious bunkers to set up an approach shot to a deliciously bunkered, ledge green cradled in the dunes of one of the bigger hills.

Little attention is usually given to the short 7th, which is a better hole for being routed up a hill rather than over an adjacent pond, while the 8th green is unreceptive, being sloped down towards the back and attendant bunkers. A mid-length par 4 follows, with a tricky pitch uphill to the green, and then comes the fabulous 10th, as wonderful a short par 4 as you could hope to find, tempting the long hitter to drive the green and punishing even the slightest failure mercilessly. It remains a great hole despite our superior clubs and balls.

▶ For tournaments, a composite course is drawn from the West and East Courses, keeping play within the boundaries of the main club grounds and avoiding road crossings.

▶ Royal Melbourne's founders included a number of Scots: John Bruce, Tom Finlay and Hugh Playfair, from St Andrews, and William Knox and Tom Brentnall from Musselburgh.

CARD OF THE COURSE

Hole	Distance (yards)	Par
1	429	4
2	480	5
3	354	4
4	470	5
5	176	3
6	428	4
7	148	3
8	379	4
9	416	4
Out	3,280	36
10	305	4
11	455	4
12	476	5
13	147	3
14	366	4
15	467	5
16	221	3
17	439	4
18	433	4
In	3,309	36
Total	6,589	72

'This is one of the great courses in the world, but there is a fear factor to it.'

NICK FALDO

Cape Kidnappers

Cape Kidnappers Golf Course, Hawke's Bay, North Island, New Zealand

For many years New Zealand has been something of a golfing sleeper. Given the natural advantages of climate and setting few courses realized their true potential, Paraparaumu Beach being one of the exceptions. Now there are two spectacular modern courses – Kauri Cliffs and Cape Kidnappers – that have raised the bar enormously, just as their American developer, Julian Robertson, has raised the bar in golf tourism in New Zealand.

The name, Cape Kidnappers, is sufficient to suggest that here are to be found stunning seascapes and any number of fabulous holes exploiting them. But the key to maximizing the potential of a site of this kind is what you do with the rest of the course. It would be disappointing to have to play dull holes on dull ground simply as a means of getting to the exceptional holes. By choosing Tom Doak as the designer, Robertson was on to a winner, for Doak is a master at routing a golf course, ensuring that every hole is of golfing interest, that there is a good balance between sorts and styles of holes and that the entire course is memorable. He and his team walked the site many times before setting to work, taking in the enormity of the task, getting to know every inch of the ground and simply coming to terms with the magnificent canvas he had been given. Doak was able to exploit his talent for locating stunning green sites.

RIGHT *On the edge of the earth, the 12th green is just one of a number of stunningly sited targets presented to the golfer during the round.*

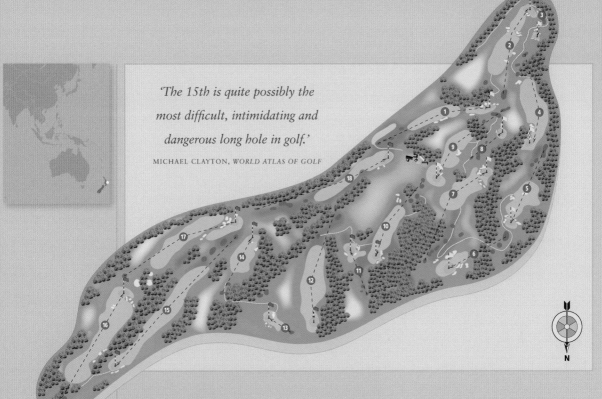

'The 15th is quite possibly the
most difficult, intimidating and
dangerous long hole in golf.'

MICHAEL CLAYTON, *WORLD ATLAS OF GOLF*

Width and options

Doak has rebelled against the 'total' architecture of many of his contemporaries: not for him narrow fairways that call for target golf on every shot. Instead, where possible, Doak gives you width, just as Alister MacKenzie did in the early 20th century. And, just as MacKenzie's greens were defended cleverly so that you had to conjure up a different kind of approach shot depending on where exactly you were on the fairway, Doak requires you to use your imagination by giving you choice.

You are, for instance, given a lovely wide fairway on the 1st, tempting you into a big drive. But the green is angled across the line of the fairway and cleverly bunkered. Unless you are in the correct part of the fairway you may find you have no shot to the green. You have to do your homework – on every hole: you cannot blast your way round here.

Cape Kidnappers would be a fine course even if it consisted solely of holes comparable with the early ones, but it is at the 12th that it becomes exceptional, with a string of breathtaking clifftop holes. And that 12th green – sitting on the skyline twixt heaven and hell! It is followed by a short hole on the very edge of the cliffs and a clever drive-and-pitch hole made particularly devilish by a demon of a pot-bunker. This gives way to a 650-yard/594-m par 5 of incredible beauty and great treachery: to the left a vertiginous drop to the ocean; to the right a ball-swallowing ravine. Although a stroke might be rescued at the 16th, the two closing holes are decidedly tough, with Doak making you think until the very last putt has dropped.

▶ In 2007 *Golf Digest* magazine rated Cape Kidnappers the 10th best course in the world outside the United States – some accolade for a course opened as recently as 2004!

▶ The name Cape Kidnappers was given to this spot in 1769 by Captain Cook following a Maori's attempt to abduct his cabin boy from his ship, HMS *Endeavour*.

CARD OF THE COURSE

Hole	Distance (yards)	Par
1	440	4
2	540	5
3	215	3
4	544	5
5	420	4
6	225	3
7	453	4
8	182	3
9	403	4
Out	3,422	35
10	430	4
11	224	3
12	460	4
13	130	3
14	348	4
15	650	5
16	500	5
17	463	4
18	480	4
In	3,685	36
Total	7,107	71

ROBERTSON'S VISION

Julian Robertson's other contribution to state-of-the-art golf in New Zealand is Kauri Cliffs on the North Island. As at Cape Kidnappers there are stunning seascapes from this clifftop course, which was laid out by David Harman, the Florida-based golf course designer. No fewer than 15 holes look out to sea, although some of the best holes are inland, such as the par-5 4th. The first skirmish with the ocean comes at the par-3 7th, an all-or-nothing carry over an abyss. There is an invigorating sequence of clifftop holes on the back nine, too, from the 14th to the 17th. Obviously, there are similarities between the two courses, because of their spectacular locations, but what makes a fascinating comparison is in the fine detail work of the two very different architects.

RIGHT *The spectacular setting of the stretch of holes from the 14th to the 17th is wonderfully captured in this aerial photograph. The 14th and 17th greens are in the foreground.*

►►► Index

Page numbers in **bold** refer to main entries

A

Alison, Hugh 54
Alliss, Peter 28
Anderson, 'Old Daw' 10
Andrade, Billy 53
Argentine Open 64, 65
Armour, Tommy 12
Augusta National **46–47**

B

Ball, John 32
Ballesteros, Severiano (Seve) 8, 31, 51, 67, 74, 76
Ballybunion **42–45**, 82
Bandon Dunes 81
Banff Springs **60–61**
Belfry, The **26–27**
Blue Canyon **88–89**
Braid, James 8, 12, 14–15, 16, 20, 23
British Amateur 8, 32, 46
British Open 8, 10, 12, 13, 16, 17, 18, 20, 22, 23, 24, 25, 29, 30, 31, 32, 33, 46

C

Cabo del Sol **62–63**
Cabrera, Angel 64
Canada Cup 35
Cape Kidnappers 7, **92–95**
Carnoustie **12–13**
Celtic Manor **38–39**
Charles, Bob 76
Clayton, Michael 93
Colt, Harry 16, 34, 35, 54
Cotton, Henry 12, 16
Couples, Fred 75
Crans-sur-Sierre **76–77**
Crenshaw, Ben 17, 20
Cruden Bay 24
Crump, George 54
Curtis Cup 34
Cypress Point 47

D

Darwin, Bernard 33
Dassù, Baldovino 76
Doak, Tom 7, 92–95
Donald, Luke 76
Dubai Desert Classic 78, 79
Duval, David 86
Dye, Pete 50, 51, 56, 57, 86

E

Eby, Stan 69
Els, Ernie 16, 17, 35, 76, 78, 79, 80, 86, 88
Emirates **78–79**

European Masters 76, 77
European Open 25
European Tour 76, 78

F

Faldo, Nick 8, 16, 68, 69, 76, 79, 86, 87, 90, 91
Fancourt **80–81**
Fiddian, Eric 41
French Open 66

G

Gallagher, Bernard 34
Ganton **28–29**
Garcia, Sergio 12, 76
German Open 69
Gleneagles **14–15**, 24
Golf Digest 53, 93

H

Hagen, Walter 16, 22
Harman, David 94
Havers, Arthur 22
Hawtree family 30
Hawtree, Martin 31
Herd, Alex 23
Hilton, Harold 32
Hogan, Ben 12, 13, 35
Hole, Frank 25
Honourable Company of Edinburgh Golfers 6, 16
Hotchkin, Neil 36
Hotchkin, Stafford Vere 36, 37

I

Interlachen 8
Irish Open 43

J

Jacklin, Tony 31
Jacobs, John 34
James II, King of Scotland 16
Jockey Club, The **64–65**
Johnnie Walker Championship (Europe) 14
Johnnie Walker Classic 88
Jones, Robert Tyre (Bobby/Bob) 8, 13, 32, 46, 47

K

Kato, Yoshikazu 88
Kauri Cliffs 92, 94
Kiawah Island **50–51**, 54
Kite, Tom 56, 57, 75

L

Lawrie, Paul 12
Le Golf National **66–67**
Leadbetter, David 86
Lee, Joe 70
Leith 16

Leonard, Justin 56
Levi, Wayne 51
Litten, Karl 78
Locke, Bobby 61, 76
Love, Davis 56
Lyle, Sandy 25

M

MacKenzie, Alister 47, 64, 65, 90, 91, 93
Maiden, Stewart 13
Martin, Bob 10
Masters, The 13, 46–47
Matthews, Sir Terry 38, 39
McClay Kidd, David 81
Merion 8
Mission Hills **86–87**
Montgomerie, Colin 39, 76, 87
Morcom, Mick 90
Morris, Old Tom 6, 7, 12, 16, 18, 40, 60
Morris, Young Tom 32
Muirfield **16–17**, 20
Muirfield Village 17

N

Nagle, Kel 76
Nicholson, Harry 76
Nicklaus, Jack 8, 14, 15, 16, 17, 23, 25, 31, 52, 53, 62, 63, 77, 80, 87
Norman, Greg 86, 88

O

Olazábal, Jose Maria 76, 86, 87
Olympic Club 42
Open Championship *see* British Open
Ortiz-Patiño, Jaime 74, 75
Ozaki, Jumbo 86, 87

P

Palmer, Arnold 22, 23, 55, 69
Park, Willie 7
Pasatiempo 47
Pebble Beach 24, 25, 46, **52–53**
PGA Championship 35
Pine Valley 26, **54–55**
Player, Gary 12, 16, 29, 34, 80–81
Powell, Thomas 38, 39
President's Cup 80
Prestwick 16, 22, 29
Professional Golfers' Association (PGA) 56

Q

Quinta do Lago 71

R

Rees, Dai 76
Robertson, Allan 7, 12
Robertson, Julian 92, 94
Romero, Eduardo 76
Ross, Donald 18
Ross, Phillip Mackenzie 25
Royal and Ancient Golf Club of St Andrews (R&A) 6, 8, 10, 11,84, 85, 90
Royal Birkdale **30–31**
Royal Blackheath 16
Royal Calcutta **84–85**
Royal Co. Down 6, **40–41**
Royal Dornoch **18–21**, 82
Royal Liverpool 9, **32–33**
Royal Melbourne **90–91**
Royal Troon **22–23**
Russell, Alex 90
Ryder Cup 14, 26, 29, 31, 34, 35, 39, 51, 74, 75

S

St Andrews 6, 8–11, 12, 16, 46, 64, 82, 90
   Links Management Trust 6
   Old Course 6, **8–11**, 16, 84
St George's Hill 34
San Lorenzo **70–73**
Sarazen, Gene 23
Scott, Adam, 56
Senior British Open 40
Simpson, Tom 16, 43
Singh, Vijay 86
Sjöland, Patrik 43

Smith, Alex 13
Smith, Macdonald 13
Smith, Willie 13
Snead, Sam 35
Sorenstam, Annika 86
Sotogrande 74
Sporting Club Berlin **68–69**
Stadler, Craig 65, 76
Stadler, Kevin 65
Steel, Donald 25, 36, 41
Strath, Andrew and David 10
Sutherland, John 18, 20
Sutton, Hal 56
Swiss Open 76

T

Tarrant, George 34
Taylor, J. H. 20, 23
Thomas, Dave 26
Thompson, Stanley 60, 61
Tissies, Hermann 23
TPC Sawgrass 64, **56–59**, 87
Travers, Jerome 54
Travis, Walter 54
Trent Jones, Robert 6, 38, 44, 74, 75
Trent Jones Jr, Robert 38
Trevino, Lee 15, 16, 31
Turnberry **24–25**

U

US Amateur 8, 46, 52
US Open 8, 13, 46, 52, 64
US PGA 86
US PGA Championship 51, 56, 58

V

Valderrama 38, **74–75**
Vale de Lobo 71
van de Velde, Jean 13
Vardon, Harry 17, 20, 23
Vicenzo, Roberto de 32
Volvo Masters 74

W

Walker Cup 40
Warren, Marc 87
Watson, Tom 12, 16, 18, 19, 25, 40, 42, 43, 44, 52
Weiskopf, Tom 62, 63
Wentworth **34–35**
Westwood, Lee 76
Wethered, Roger 8
Wilson, Hugh 54
Wind, Herbert Warren 19
Woodhall Spa **36–37**
Woods, Tiger 8, 9, 13, 32, 33, 47, 52, 56, 78, 79, 80, 88, 89
Woosnam, Ian 39, 76, 78
World Cup of Golf (formerly Canada Cup) 86, 87
World Matchplay 35

Acknowledgements

The publishers would like to thank the following for permission to reproduce copyright material:

Celtic Manor Resort, p 38.

Corbis/Tony Roberts, p 63.

Getty Images, p 48; /David Alexander, pp 8, 9, 78; /Stan Badz/PGA, p 58; /David Cannon, pp 2, 6, 6–7, 7, 14, 16, 18, 19, 22, 24, 34, 36, 40, 41, 42, 60, 61, 76, 90, 92, 94–95; /Chris Condon/PGA, p 56; /Richard Heathcote, p86; /Harry How, pp 48–49, 49, 52; /Image Source Black, p 4–5; /Ross Kinnaird, p 58–59; /Warren Little, pp 66, 67; /Steve Munday, p 28.

Kiawah Island Golf Resort, pp 50, 51.

Iain Lowe Photography, p 20–21.

Brian Morgan, pp 62, 84, 85.

Ran Morrissett/GolfClubAtlas.com, p 90.

Phil Sheldon Golf Picture Library, pp 26, 27, 30, 44–45, 46, 54, 55, 80; /Liz Anthony, pp 10–11, 12, 32; /Richard Castka, pp 86 above, 89; /Karina Hoskyns, pp 72–73, 73.

Stefan von Stengel pp 68, 69, 70, 74, 82, 82–83, 88.